PERSPECTIVES ON RACE AND COMMUNITY

in the Lehigh Valley

A publication by college and university students

2021
Writing Wrongs

The mission of Writing Wrongs is to generate awareness and promote understanding of various social issues by providing an immersion experience for student multimedia journalists. They produce an entire print book and media about the specified topic in one weekend.

Copyright ©2023 Writing Wrongs: Milena Berestko, Jennifer Berrios, Sonjirose Chin, Tiersa Curry, Natalie Dang, Veronika Hammond, Shanaé Harte, Kelly Sulca Hernandez, Benjamin Hopper, Ian Long, Jesse Marsh, Luka Marjanovic, Heather Moran, Alliana Myers, Chukwudiebube Nwaeme, Shannon O'Connor, Chekwubechi Okunowo, Catherine Oriel, Rohail Spear, Kylie Stoltzfus, Doris Turkel

All image rights reserved.

All rights reserved. No parts of this book may be reproduced, in any form, without permission from the publisher, except for a reviewer who wishes to quote brief passages.

Book designed in Adobe InDesign.
Fonts: Nantes by Luzi Gantenbein, Adrianna by Chank Diesel, and Revolt by Sam Rowe.

The views in this book are those of the authors and individuals and do not necessarily reflect the opinions or policies of the organizations or institutions included, mentioned, or advertised in the publication.

Published by
New Dawn Enterprises, LLC

Contact
P.O. Box 654
Kutztown, PA 19530
dawn@seekreporttruth.com

Social
@seekreporttruth
@seek_report_truth

Web
seekreporttruth.com

TABLE OF CONTENTS

Letter From the Editor 1

Racism Through Different Lenses. 2

Sowing Seeds of Community 9

Seedfolks: A Community Garden Brings Transformation 11

The Importance of Connection 13

Mistakes and Moving On... 18

Stuck Between Two Worlds. 20

Be Your Authentic Self 22

Nigerian History: A Tool For Racial Justice 25

Don't Quit. Keep Going. 27

A Path of Perseverance and Passion 30

Murder, Ministry, and Misdiagnosis: The Story of Veronica James. 33

Renewed Perspective...35

The Great Commission...37

Bringing the Boogie-Down Bronx to the Lehigh Valley 41

Grit and Resilience:
An Evolution of the Black Church in the Lehigh Valley 43

Innocence and Revelation: The Moravian Community of Bethlehem.........47

A Man With a Heart for Stories 52

Us, The Dreamers..55

Setting A Precedent..58

Black Lives Matter: In Remembrance 60

2021 Writing Wrongs Staff 62

2021 Writing Wrongs Advisors 64

Timeline Notes 70

LETTER FROM THE EDITOR

Since 2015, Writing Wrongs has hosted journalism programs for college students to report on social issues through gathering the stories of those directly affected. The students travel to the designated community, interview and photograph residents, and compile their stories into a print book with the goal of raising awareness and offering the public a better understanding of these issues. All work must be completed during the Labor Day weekend program. We have never worked on a book after the program ended, because students return to their respective schools and continue their academic and other responsibilities, and the advisors go back to their professional and personal lives as well. Time and location constraints would make it extremely difficult to complete the book after the program.

The 2021 program on Sept. 3 – 6 proved this rule to be necessary.

Hurricane Ida hit Louisiana on August 29 and traveled north, reaching Pennsylvania, New York, and New Jersey on September 1. Even though it had been reclassified as a post-tropical cyclone by then, Ida still caused extensive power outages, flooded streets, and road blocks. Many of the students were traveling from New York City and New Jersey where public transit was at a standstill. Students arrived late to the program and the Friday evening orientation was cut short. Still, they could refer to numerous documents from the summer orientation segment regarding work in their respective fields at the program: writing/editing, photography, print design, videography, and social media management. Advisors were available for any questions.

The weekend proceeded as usual. The student multimedia journalists interviewed community members at the program's Bethlehem location and traveled to other locations for interviews. The print design team worked on the layout and book cover. Social media managers posted updates to Writing Wrongs' social media accounts.

After the weekend concluded and the stories were reviewed, it became apparent that more work would be needed prior to publishing. Two of our board members met with the writers several times, virtually, to revise their work. Because of individual schedules, this took some time.

Instead of devoting extra time and resources to publish, we could have chosen to abandon the book. However, two years later, these stories are still relevant and worth sharing. The intensive work of both the students and advisors who volunteered to participate should be honored, as well as the people who so openly shared their lived experiences with us as catalysts for change.

It is important to keep in mind while reading the stories that they were written two years ago. I hope that you will share your thoughts by leaving a review on the website through which you purchased it.

Yours in progress,

Dawn Heinbach, M.A.
Independent Multimedia Journalist

Staff Writer Ebube Nwaeme describes the cultural differences between Nigeria and the U.S. regarding racism. Bethlehem, Pa., Sept. 4, 2021. (Writing Wrongs/Shannon O'Connor)

RACISM IN THE USA

1492

Christopher Columbus (1451–1506) lands on an island in the Bahamas and claims it as Spanish territory. Believing that he had found Asia, he calls the native Taino people "Indians." His arrival in this "new world" initiates European colonization in the West.[1] By 1514, the Taino population of Hispaniola (Haiti) has dwindled from more than approximately 7 million to just 22,000 as a result of disease, massacre, and the inhumane conditions of slavery.[2]

RACISM THROUGH DIFFERENT LENSES

Talking to the Writing Wrongs Staff

By Shanaé Harte

One of the first things people are made aware of as a child is the color of their skin. While still learning about their race as they grow, some children are taught how to deal with issues that may arise because of their race, some are taught about an established racial hierarchy, and some are taught nothing.

Growing up in a predominantly Asian community in southern California kept 26-year-old **Natalie Dang** in a bubble that did not allow for any form of racism. For most of her life, she was surrounded by children and adults that looked like her, so she never thought about being seen as different. It was not until she grew older that she began to notice microaggressions toward her and the feeling of being different and discriminated against became a constant occurrence.

The first instance of overt racism happened on what was supposed to be a regular day. As she stood in a pharmacy, a white woman approached her and repeatedly yelled at her to return to her home country. Dang is American. At this moment, Dang thought, "Are you sure you want to do this right now?" because other native-Asians worked in that pharmacy. The strange occurrence prohibited her from even thinking of herself and the fact that she was the one being placed in a dangerous situation.

In another instance, while at a prior boyfriend's house, Dang was relaxing when the doorbell rang. A family member opened the door, maybe expecting a food delivery or a friendly face, but instead she was greeted by children who began to mock her for her appearance. The joke, to these children, was that this woman at the door was Asian. The woman's fight or flight response did not effectuate. Instead, she froze. She was teased, laughed at, and made fun of. Not only did these children tease this woman whom they had never met, but after having their "fun," they walked away from the scene leaving her broken. To make matters worse, the children left the scene with a sense of normalcy, as if they had done nothing wrong. The two painful sides of this story are one woman being taunted for something that was not a choice and children thinking it was okay to tease her. This belief that these children hold was not instilled in them at birth; this was, presumably, taught.

"These are things that people shouldn't have to deal with," said Dang. She believes that some people would see this situation and attribute it to "kids being kids." But Dang said the attitude of the children was likely taught. "Who taught them to do that? ... Those [are] experiences

1513 Spanish explorer Juan Ponce de Leon (1474–1521) lands on the east coast of North America. He explores the islands and west coast of this peninsula he names Florida. On a return trip in 1521, he and his crew are attacked by Native Americans. De Leon is severely wounded and dies later in Cuba.[3]

1539 Hernando de Soto (1500–1542) lands in Tampa Bay, Florida and explores the south, traveling across what is now Alabama, Georgia, the Carolinas, Tennessee, and Alabama. The party is consistently attacked by Native Americans. De Soto is the first explorer to cross the Mississippi River.[4]

Staff Writer Natalie Dang strolls through the historic grounds of the Moravian Cemetery on Saturday, Sept. 4, 2021. Bethlehem, Pa. (Writing Wrongs/Shannon O'Connor)

people shouldn't have, but also, the younger generations need to be taught," said Dang.

Shortly after the COVID-19 pandemic began, there was a rise in anti-Asian hate crimes as many people, including then-President Donald Trump, associated COVID-19 with Asians. Reports of Asian-Americans and native-Asians being spit on, struck, and even killed flooded the news. The idea that racism also includes Asians became more recognizable. While society was aware that racism towards the Asian community existed, when people speak about racism it is mostly referencing the Black and white communities. Therefore, Dang often felt like she could not tell where she and other Asians fit into the issue of race. As these hate crimes towards her community increased, she eventually fell into an identity crisis where she found herself asking questions like, "What does racism mean to Asians?" Her feelings constantly changed from worry and confusion to irritation and anger. Fear flooded her mind as the uncertainty of her family's fate grew.

"It makes me angry because these people are so cowardly that they're going after [the elderly]," said Dang.

Her empathy toward elderly people like her grandparents is partly because she sees them as defenseless. "It's one of those things, like, pick on someone your own size, you know?"

The increase in anti-Asian hate crimes quickly caught the attention of the government and an anti-Asian hate crime bill was soon passed by the U.S. House of Representatives. While the bill cannot prevent these crimes from occurring, the Asian community was given the assurance that their issues were being heard. Additionally, there are now more open spaces for this community to report and document any issues that may transpire. Despite the efforts of the government and other third parties, Dang believes that many members of her community are still fearful to speak up about any negative experience they have encountered, but she implores them to continue to raise awareness of any hate directed toward Asians so that protection is always offered where needed.

Unlike Dang, who was in a societal bubble from a young age, **Ebube Nwaeme**, a native Nigerian, was exposed to colorism, which Oxford Dictionary describes as "prejudice or discrimination against individuals with a dark skin tone, typically among people of the same ethnic or racial group." Many believe colorism is a variant of racism. In Nigeria, some people consider racism to be an epidemic as many natives conduct cosmetic measures to make their skin appear lighter. Therefore, Nwaeme was accustomed to classist discrimination. Even though Nwaeme understood colorism and racism, he always found it difficult to associate these negative factors with his country.

Nwaeme said, "It's very difficult to think about it [in a negative] way because out there, we just live our lives. We don't know when things happen with one another." Nevertheless, he admitted that racial stereotypes exist and do sometimes cause a divide between the Yoruba and Hausa tribes in Nigeria. "I don't know if we have racism, but I would say colorism is more prominent."

The confusion of the existence of racism vanished once Nwaeme migrated to the United States. "It hit me pretty hard, to be honest, because this is stuff I [didn't] know about," he said.

Because he was vaguely oblivious to true racism, it took a while for Nwaeme to recognize microaggressions and stereotypes directed toward him. "Looking back at all the stuff that happened to me in high school, I'm thinking, 'Wow. That was low-key racist.'"

Besides stereotypical prejudice and microaggressions, Nwaeme has not personally encountered any of the typically overt forms of racism but finds himself being extra careful based on public experiences and experiences of other Black friends.

One particular incident that stays in the back of Nwaeme's mind was an instance where two of his Black friends were accused of stealing an electronic delivery bike and were forced to spend a night in jail based on assumption. Just this one occurrence has caused him to become more reserved when he is in public so that he does not appear as the stereotypical young Black man.

"It just shows that you're way closer to these things than you actually think you are," Nwaeme said. "You just have to be worried sometimes about being more reserved or trying to be low-key just so that you don't get into these situations."

Thinking about police brutality or general anti-Black hate crimes pushes Nwaeme to act in unusual ways to ensure his safety. For instance, if walking alone on a winter night, he won't pull his hoodie up so that no one will have a reason to approach him, as cold as it may be. Even on his way to the 2021 Writing Wrongs program, he felt the need to tell soldiers who were patrolling the train station that he was walking by them frequently because he wanted to ensure he was going to the correct train. Instead of being able to concentrate on his journey to Bethlehem, Pennsylvania, he was anxious about being targeted, like Oscar Grant.

As a black man and an immigrant, Nwaeme believes that government officials should be doing more for the Black community. President Joe Biden received a lot of negative press during his campaign after saying that Black people were not Black if they did not cast a vote for him. While people were upset with his choice of words,

> "Many believe that colorism is a variant of racism."

Staff Writer Natalie Dang. Bethlehem, Pa., Sept. 4, 2021. (Writing Wrongs/Jennifer Berrios)

1619 Twenty enslaved Africans are brought to Virginia. The ship's captain trades with the colonists, exchanging the human cargo for food and supplies. This is the first transaction in what eventually develops into an extensive system of chattel slavery in North America.[7]

Staff Writer Ebube Nwaeme. Bethlehem, Pa., Sept. 4, 2021. (Writing Wrongs/Jennifer Berrios)

they were also curious to see if, finally, significant changes would be made. President Biden, during his campaign, said to Black voters, "You've always had my back, and I'll have yours." Thus far, this has not been the case. Yes, we have had a few remorseful words when something was made public, but words are just words. Where is the action?

"There's a lot that can be done. I work with youth and I try to make them aware of resources that are being provided by the government, but I can't teach you [about] anything if there's nothing available for you," Nwaeme said.

One common factor between Nwaeme and Dang is that they both did not have substantial conversations about racism and were forced to learn about it in the moment. Recently, Idaho, Arkansas, and Florida, among other states, have begun to ban the teaching of Critical Race Theory as well as African American history in schools. Both Nwaeme and Dang believe that the lack of education on racism would hurt society; there would be a reverse in history. Though Dang did not have conversations about racism when she was younger, she believes that this should not be the case for younger generations and strongly disagrees with removing these teachings from schools.

"It's important to teach what really happened in history because a lot of the things we are taught are only from one perspective and there's never just one side to a story," said Dang. "I'm still trying to understand why people are so against teaching kids these different perspectives. … Just be more transparent about history."

While Ebube Nwaeme is on board for education on Critical Race Theory and racism, he also feels it is crucial that the person delivering the teachings is someone to whom the student can relate. "I'm just going to be honest. I don't know how a white man could teach me about racism. I don't know if that makes sense," Nwaeme said.

Whether conversations about race happen in school or at home, there's no doubt that they need to happen. The importance of education on race is evident in the case of **Luka Marjanovic**, who was born and raised in Bosnia where "there are no real race issues." While he was aware of racism because of racial injustices between Bosnians and Romani people, when he thought of the U.S., he believed that the issue of racism was completely eradicated. And the race issue between Bosnians and Romani people, according to him, is not as extensive as racism issues between white people and other races in the U.S.

"I knew what racism was towards Black people and how the United States functioned from a distance, but I never had a strong opinion on it," said Marjanovic.

The distance and lack of education caused Marjanovic to believe that racism was "fixed" because of Black people attaining various positions of power. Seeing Barack Obama become President confirmed his theory that racism no longer existed in the U.S.

"I was against racism, but I thought it was gone," he said.

It was not until Marjanovic moved to the U.S. and was surrounded by new types of people that he realized his thinking about racism was wrong, so this was something he sought to change. Because of his past ignorance, he wishes that there were more conversations and educational lessons about racism.

"We talked about racism, but the way in which we talked about it was mostly … historically based," Marjanovic said. "We talked about slavery; we talked about the Civil War, and that seemed to make it like a thing of the past because it's a part of history. That was something I was mistaken about."

In this case, Marjanovic knew that racism was wrong and was against it, but he was still oblivious to the fact that the epidemic still existed. Now, just stop to imagine how ignorant a child who is not taught about Critical Race Theory or African American history may eventually be? Especially in the United States, imagine the irreversible effects a lack of education on racism would have on society.

1661

The first anti-miscegenation law is enacted in Maryland. These laws ban marriage between white and Black people primarily, but also include other non-white groups such as Native Americans and Asians. In some states, the ban criminalizes cohabitation and sex between these racial groups. Anti-miscegenation laws inevitably become widespread in the United States, especially in the South.[8]

Marjanovic confronted his ignorance, learned about existing issues, and is now using his voice to educate others who may be like his past self.

"I wish we talked about [racism] more because that affects us directly," he said, referencing education on the topic in Bosnia. "I've seen ignorant people who, like me, thought that racism was not an issue anymore, which is equally distressing and it's just slowing down progress."

Marjanovic has now made it a mission to be an ally where needed and is using his voice in various ways, including through Writing Wrongs' 2021 program, to raise awareness for those who may not be able to do so on their own.

This case is only one instance of why the topic of racism should not be ignored or hidden. There is no assurance that there will be positive developments in eradicating racism as early as desired, but these stories are reminders as to why changes need to be made sooner rather than later. Change will not come unless actions are put into place.

While we wait for these developments to be made, Natalie Dang and Ebube Nwaeme are encouraging their communities to be triumphant over the hate they may be currently experiencing — in whatever way that may be. For Dang, as much as the ignorance and arrogance of racism pains her, she refuses to allow hate and negative energy to infiltrate her being. Likewise, Ebube implores members of his community to disregard stereotypes and not live up to the expectations that have been cast on Black people because of race.

"Don't try to prove them wrong. Try to prove yourself right," said Nwaeme.

Discussions with Dang, Nwaeme, and Marjanovic uncovered that racism is a complex issue — there is more to it than just being Asian, Black, or white. Therefore, to make positive advancements in society concerning race, change must begin with each individual.

From his home country of Bosnia-Herzegovena, Staff Writer Luka Marjanovic believed that racism in the U.S. was a thing of the past. While attending college in New Jersey, he discovered that racism is still very much a part of American culture. Bethlehem, Pa., Sept. 4, 2021. (Writing Wrongs/Alliana Myers)

1756

The French and Indian War, also known as the Seven Years War, begins over land claims in North America, namely the Ohio and Mississippi Valleys. France and Great Britain both have explored and established a presence in these territories, but the Native Americans have stronger alliances with the French. The war ends with the Treaty of Paris of 1863, granting Britain more land and allowing increased European expansion in the West.[9]

Michael Richardson, staff member at Promise Neighborhoods of the Lehigh Valley, holds his Bulldog puppy Hazel while standing between rows of peppers and other vegetables at The Seed Farm. Emmaus, Pa., Sept. 4, 2021. (Writing Wrongs/Alliana Myers)

1787

At the Constitutional Convention in Philadelphia, slavery is one of several issues on the agenda and is hotly debated. Georgia and South Carolina refuse to entertain the idea of eliminating their source of free labor; their economies depend on it. The delegates of the convention deny Congress the power to end the Atlantic slave trade for another 20 years.[10] On the same day, the Fugitive Slave Clause is added to the Constitution. This clause states that even if an enslaved person flees to a state where slavery is illegal, this does not grant them freedom and they must be returned to their owners.[11]

SOWING SEEDS OF COMMUNITY

By Doris Turkel

At the top of a hill in Emmaus, Pennsylvania, eight rows of colorful vegetables sit adjacent to a rustic red farmhouse. With seven-week-old American bulldog Hazel at his heels, Michael Richardson greeted us with a smile, wearing a hand-made shirt that read "End Gun Violence." As a Black farmer in rural Pennsylvania, Richardson has devoted himself to uplifting others through agricultural activism and education. Richardson is naturally charismatic and friendly, and his energy was palpable as he led us over to his plot at The Seed Farm, a local farm business incubator, to show off his crops and tell his story.

As Hazel rolled in the mud at our feet and happily ate whole tomatoes off the vine, Richardson gushed about his garden and the ways in which it allows him to help and foster communities in the Lehigh Valley. However, having a garden was never in Richardson's plans.

"I'm from Brooklyn, New York. I'm 46 years old. I grew up in the crack epidemic. So being able to do this, and to be giving back to the community ... knowing that I was part of some of the wrongs of the community — it feels so good," Richardson said.

As a teen, Richardson was moved from Brooklyn to the Poconos by his mother. After getting into some legal trouble and serving time in prison, Richardson found his niche — agriculture, which came naturally to him, as both his mother and grandmother were avid growers.

Richardson hopes to share the transformative experience that agriculture provided him with others of similar backgrounds. "When I talk to people like me, I am able to give them a message and show them that with the right mindset you can be something so much more than what they try to make you to be — a number in the system," he explained. "We are so much more than a piece of paper." To avoid falling victim to the lasting dehumanization of incarceration, Richardson encourages independence and productivity through hard work.

In addition to frequently donating fresh produce to halfway houses, Richardson's experience in the criminal justice system has motivated him to

1793

The second United States Congress passes the Fugitive Slave Act, which provides stronger enforcement measures to the previous Fugitive Slave Clause. It guarantees the rights of enslavers to track and capture their human property if they escape into another state or federal territory. The Act's provisions for proof of ownership are lax; an oral statement will suffice. No time constraint is included, so formerly enslaved escapees can be caught and returned to slavery many years later. People who interfere with the return of an enslaver's property face financial penalties.[12]

begin his own startup, "Everyone Deserves Housing." With a plot of land he has in the Poconos, he hopes to provide temporary housing to those in need or to those who have been liberated from incarceration, and help them find jobs in the area.

In every endeavor, Richardson encourages youth and locals to find something they enjoy and work towards a goal, whether athletic, artistic, or agricultural. Aside from running his garden and founding his non-profit, Richardson breeds and trains emotional support dogs, coaches basketball, and works with children on projects like screen printing and clothing design through Promise Neighborhoods of Lehigh Valley (PNLV).

Richardson has been living in Allentown since 2015, and has been a volunteer for PNLV since 2017. Promise Neighborhoods is an organization that gives children and families in different areas of Pennsylvania access to educational programs and opportunities. Richardson had just become an official employee of PNLV when he rented his plot of land from The Seed Farm, a farm business incubator with which PNLV partners. He planted his first harvest in February.

Richardson's farm boasts green peppers, broccoli, cabbage, basil, tomatoes, cherry tomatoes, and purple kale. While many of the other farmers at The Seed Farm sell their produce to grocery stores or run their own businesses, Richardson's garden is completely not for profit. Almost all of Richardson's fresh vegetables go straight to local food banks or halfway homes, under the guidance of Second Harvest Food Bank of the Lehigh Valley. "We grow stuff for the community. Once we harvest, we take it to food banks and food lines in the community; we drop off what we grew. That feeling alone is beautiful," Richardson said.

The Second Harvest Food Bank works with over 200 agencies in the area to gather and distribute food donations from places like Richardson's garden. Second Harvest works in conjunction with The Seed Farm. The Seed Farm trains, supplies machinery to, and provides business and marketing support for new farmers and aspiring agricultural business owners so that people like Richardson can grow and manage their own produce.

What motivates Richardson's work at The Seed Farm is community, a value that has shaped his life. From growing up in the housing projects in Brooklyn to working with Promise Neighborhoods, Richardson described the importance of people coming together to help and care for each other. Richardson brings young people from the Lehigh Valley to The Seed Farm to teach them about planting and the self-sufficiency that is gained from it. His garden has volunteers, and interns work throughout the season to learn how to harvest their own crops.

Although Richardson recently began his agricultural expedition, he feels a sense of pride for his work at The Seed Farm that triumphs over any obstacles he may face. "Me being the way I am, dressed the way I am, people may still look down on me because I have a felony, but I know that I'm still doing good, so I'm cool with that," he said. Richardson acknowledges past wrongdoings but lives in the present, and puts his energy towards a future in which more people enjoy the benefits of agriculture and an overall higher quality of life, emphasizing that "everybody does wrong, so judging me for what I've done in the past and paid my dues for is wrong. This makes everything right for me."

For Richardson, his farm is also about family. He frequently brings his six children to the farm to help him tend to the crops and learn about agriculture. Richardson joked, "I just brought my 13-year-old son up with me — he likes basketball more than farming." Richardson is also a passionate cook and uses his fresh produce to make homemade meals for his family of eight.

When asked what he wants people to gain from working at his plot, Richardson said, "I'm hoping that people learn how to grow their own food, take care of themselves, and not depend on going to the supermarket. Or if they don't have money, they can come together and start growing their own crops." This is not only an agricultural goal for Richardson, but representative of his general philosophy. For Richardson, agriculture extends beyond its nourishing qualities, providing a sense of personal accomplishment to those involved and creating a network of aid through food and work. Richardson strongly believes that "if you come together and get your own plot somewhere, you can feed enough people to sustain a community." He hopes to hold classes at his garden, encouraging self-sufficiency and the joys that come from growing food for oneself and others.

"It's not hard at all: It's a seed, some water, some sun, and some time," Richardson said. "To watch something grow from nothing to those beautiful peppers over there, and then being able to harvest it and cook it for yourself ... you don't have to depend on anybody."

Editor's note: *For more information about The Seed Farm, visit www.theseedfarm.org.*

1805 The Louisiana Purchase expands American territory west of the Mississippi River. Meriwether Lewis and William Clark are commissioned by the U.S. government to explore and map the newly acquired land. They hire French-Canadian fur trader Toussaint Charbonneau as an interpreter and guide. His wife Sacagawea (1788-1812), a Lemhi Shoshone woman, helps guide the expedition primarily through the Rocky Mountains in what is now Montana and Idaho.[13]

Editor's note: Staff Writers Doris Turkel and Milena Berestko visited The Seed Farm and decided to each write their own story.

SEEDFOLKS:
A Community Garden Brings Transformation

By Milena Berestko

With a smile on his face, a baseball cap representing the Promise Neighborhoods of Lehigh Valley (PNLV), and a small Pitbull/French Bulldog mix trotting close by his legs, Michael Richardson greeted us and introduced his four-legged companion, Hazel. He led us to his vegetable garden where he began telling his story.

"I am a father of six. I am a husband. I am a Black man. I am a great-grandson to Hubert Harris and a grandson of Virgil Richardson," he said, showing his land. "I am here to help my community and I enjoy helping my community. I do that for the love of it."

Richardson did not have an easy upbringing. His mother uprooted him from New York City and moved to the Pocono Mountains to save him from "trouble." At 19, he met Dr. Hasshan Batts, the director of PNLV. "He changed his life, which caused me to change my life," Richardson shared. "If it wasn't for Dr. Batts, I would not be able to [harvest crops]." He added that it would simply be impossible for him to lead a community garden if he was still in Brooklyn.

"I always thought I was a little different than everyone else because I had a chance to experience different things at a young age," Richardson said. He served time in jail and was racially profiled on multiple occasions — both experiences being the direct result of the prison-to-school pipeline and racist sentiment in the city of New York. Richardson's school and private life were drastically different. His neighborhood was over-policed while his school was a safe haven due to its prevalent white demographic.

"School was a dream as I got to get away from Brooklyn and take a train to Manhattan," he said, emphasizing that he was "gone from the projects" and always trying to spend a night at somebody else's house. "But I had to go back home and deal with pissy elevators and crackheads. It was always up and down."

Richardson was raised in public housing, maneuvering the "luxurious world of opportunities," as he called it, and "pissy elevators." His childhood taught him how to strike a balance and leave things in the past. He kept a hopeful tone. Few can communicate their life lessons with such poise.

"I grew up in the '80s. My friends was dying around me before I was a teenager." Richardson interrupted his train of thought to stop Hazel from eating a rotten tomato. "I don't miss the city. I got kids to raise out here," he continued. "I would not want my kids to live in the situation I was living. Out here, it just feels safer: You don't hear sirens all the time. You don't hear gunshots."

New York shaped his worldview. He sees the garden as his way to help others like him, the ex-strugglers, no matter how people look at him: "Being part of the

1808
The international slave trade is banned by Congress. The buying and selling of Black humans continues domestically.[14] Approximately 400,000 enslaved Africans have already been transported to America. By 1860, 4 million Africans are enslaved, comprising 13% of the U.S. population.[15, 16]

community feels so good to me and even though some people might look down on me because of my felony, I know I am still doing good, so I am cool with that."

Richardson began volunteering with Promise Neighborhoods of the Lehigh Valley in 2017 and returned as an employee in February of 2021. He spoke about the recent training he received to use farm machinery safely. They have also organized an event, called More Life, at which local vendors, independent fitness trainers, and yogis gather at Richardson's garden. He provides pallets of food to the local attendees.

Yet this is not where Richardson plans to stop his community work. He recently launched a non-profit organization to provide temporary housing and job offers for other ex-felons. Everyone Deserves Housing is a tribute to his life struggles and observations. "I know somebody who was working 40 hours a week and living in a motel with his two kids. It doesn't make sense to me," he said.

His work centers on community development and assistance, creating opportunities and a safe space for people in the Lehigh Valley.

"I would not want my kids to experience constant police presence, being frisked going to school, bars on school windows," Richardson said. "I would not want my kids to experience seeing drug use, drug dealing. This is what I see when I look at my childhood."

His four daughters and two sons are his hope. "We need more strong women," he said, and we chuckled. Richardson truly changed his life by helping the community. When he spoke about cooking as a practice requiring much imagination, when he described the fruity-pebble meatloaf and honey-nut cheerios mac and cheese he made for his children, his eyes shined. He seemed proud of where he has gone in his life. It is evident that he has a clear vision for what he wants his community to look like. He was able to visualize a life better than the one he led in New York City. With his wife, six children, and a community garden, his vision is simple: You can be more than your past mistakes.

"I want my legacy to be to just think that everything is possible," Richardson said. "If everybody works together, everything could work out."

You can be more than your past mistakes.

Michael Richardson's community work includes efforts to eradicate gun violence and assisting formerly incarcerated individuals with reentry. Emmaus, Pa., Sept. 4, 2021. (Writing Wrongs/Alliana Myers)

1830

President Andrew Jackson signs the Indian Removal Act into law. This legislation facilitates an "exchange" of Native-owned land in the cotton belt and U.S. land acquired in the Louisiana Purchase. From 1831 to 1839, tribes are forced to walk thousands of miles to what is now Oklahoma, often without food, water, and proper protection from the elements. This network of routes becomes knows as the Trail of Tears. It encompasses more than 5,000 miles through 9 states: Alabama, Arkansas, Georgia, Illinois, Kentucky, Missouri, North Carolina, Oklahoma, and Tennessee. Tens of thousands of Native Americans die on this journey, including more than 5,000 Cherokee people.[17]

Staff Writer Heather Moran (right on computer screen) interviews Tyrone Russell using Zoom. Bethlehem, Pa., Sept. 4, 2021. (Writing Wrongs/Jennifer Berrios)

THE IMPORTANCE OF CONNECTION

By Heather Moran

Tyrone Russell is an accomplished entrepreneur and an engaged community member from Allentown, Pennsylvania. He is the founder and CEO of marketing firm Faces International and the president and co-owner of the Cleveland School of Cannabis (CSC), an online and residential school for adults that teaches its students about the different aspects of the emerging cannabis industry. Russell has an impressive resume not just because of his career success but because it has always coexisted with his commitment to community.

Russell was raised by a strong single mother in San Diego, California. His mother faced some challenges, and life was tumultuous. The family moved frequently. Russell attended eleven schools by the time he graduated from high school, but he credits his mother with easing those disruptions and modeling a positive outlook.

"She showed us what it meant to live in a community no matter where we went. She was accepting of everyone," Russell said. "And, you know, I think moving from place to place and seeing how she kind of lived her life and the responsibility she gave me early on, all contributed to how

1838

Frederick Douglass (1818-1895) escapes from slavery and becomes an author and abolitionist. His autobiography, "Narrative of the Life of Frederick Douglass, An American Slave," is his first published work in 1845. He also founds and publishes the abolitionist newspaper, "The North Star." His speech at a meeting organized by the Rochester, New York Ladies' Anti-Slavery Society in 1852 becomes well-known as "What to a Slave is the Fourth of July?"[18]

> Many opponents of critical race theory lack a true understanding of it.

I live today — the feeling of being able to get into a space, a new space, and not always have to play the same role."

Still, life was not easy for Russell. Conflict between Black and Mexican students in his California high school was constant, and Russell found himself involved in confrontations that sometimes turned violent. He credits two women, whom he met when he was eight, for helping to change the trajectory of his life. Their support over the years fostered a trusting relationship, and Russell wisely accepted their influence when they suggested he move to New York state to live with them. His mother and younger brother followed a couple of months later.

Russell was a naturally gifted athlete who enjoyed playing football and basketball, and when someone suggested he run track, he decided to give that a try too. His adaptability, born out of always being the new kid, gave Russell a measure of self-awareness and self-confidence that allowed him to fill different roles in his many different schools. This flexibility, he says, followed him into his adult life.

It would be easy for people who think that systemic racism doesn't exist, or even that racism is a thing of the past, to look at someone like Russell as proof that Black men just need to work hard to become successful. Russell's response to this argument is emphatic.

"When we start talking about racism not existing and all this stuff, because Russell made it, I'm like, you got to look at Russell's entire life because the world that I was living in and the opportunities that I had aren't granted to everyone," he said. "And I have so many stories of people who weren't able to get out of the situation that I was taken out of, not because of anything that we'd done, but because of the world that was structured around us."

In his book, "The Souls of Black Folk" (1903), prominent Black sociologist W.E.B. Dubois described what it was like to be a Black man in America at the turn of the 20th century. He used the term "double-consciousness" to describe the "two-ness" a Black man feels in society as an American man and a Black man. Dubois describes this as the presence of "two warring ideals in one dark body" and the desire to combine them into one "truer self."

Dubois writes, "In this merging he wishes neither of the older selves to be lost. ... He simply wishes to make it possible for a man to be both a Negro and an American without being cursed and spit upon by his fellows, without having the doors of opportunity closed roughly in his face."

Much has changed in the United States, but the doors of opportunity are still not fully open to all. Racism continues to exist in the U.S. Its citizens are divided not only on the understanding of the magnitude of the inequity that results from racism's systemic nature but even on its very existence. The backlash against Critical Race Theory (CRT) exemplifies this divide.

Many opponents of Critical Race Theory lack a true understanding of it. The Brookings Institution, a public policy organization, explains that CRT "states that U.S. social institutions (e.g., the criminal justice system, education system, labor market, housing market, and healthcare system) are laced with racism embedded in laws, regulations, rules, and procedures that lead to differential outcomes by race." An introductory level college course in sociology gives a general historical overview of many of the racist policies that have existed and continue to exist in U.S. society. Black, Indigenous and people of color in the United States can describe how those policies impact their own lives.

Russell acknowledges that the privileges in his life — his mother, his ability to adapt to his constantly shifting surroundings, his connection to the women he befriended, and his athleticism — helped him graduate from high school and move on to college instead of ending up in jail for murder at the age of thirteen, like a young friend of his. Russell describes himself as being "extremely privileged" despite his frequent moves, experience in public housing, and attendance at public schools that were products of inequitable funding.

Russell attended Colgate University, a small, selective liberal arts college in Hamilton, New York, on an athletic scholarship. He earned a bachelor's degree in sociology in 2003. In 2008, he completed a master's degree in College Student Personnel and Counseling at Shippensburg University in Shippensburg, Pennsylvania.

Russell's self-awareness and his ability to thrive, despite the systemic racism that permeates U.S. society, has informed his personal and professional life. According to his LinkedIn

1846

The Mexican-American War begins as President James K. Polk seeks to expand U.S. borders after the annexation of Texas from Mexico one year earlier. Abolitionists view this war as an attempt by slave states to expand their territory. After a U.S. victory in 1848, the Treaty of Guadalupe Hidalgo ensures the acquisition of more than 500,000 square miles of land west of the Rio Grande to the Pacific Ocean, which today are the states of New Mexico, Utah, Arizona, California, Texas, and western Colorado.[20]

profile, his early jobs included working as the Residence Director at Shippensburg University and the Residence Life Coordinator at Lehigh University in Bethlehem, Pennsylvania. He served as the Director of Multicultural Affairs at Lehigh University from 2011 to 2015. During this time, he was also working for a nonprofit community action organization whose mission was to improve the lives of young men, and co-founded a nonprofit youth mentoring program called R2C2. The seed for Faces International — his marketing, advertising, and development company — was also planted during this time frame.

Russell's background in sociology and his own personal experiences with poverty have given him insights into the problems that arise when outsiders try to come into what they consider a needy community and "fix" it. On his LinkedIn page, he tells the story of walking through a neighborhood with an executive of a nonprofit whose organization had used donations to fund and install abstract bike racks, in the shape of the number 7, in the neighborhood. Russell, trying to make the case for involving the community in the decision-making process regarding the needs of their neighborhood, used the bike racks to help make his point.

Russell told the man that the majority of people who lived in the neighborhood didn't know that the bike racks were bike racks and, to back this up, they informally surveyed the people on the street. He recalled that only about 1 in 15 community members knew that the installations were bike racks. The others thought they were signs or simply had no idea what their purpose was. The organization had installed them without any kind of introduction.

While Russell conceded that the bike racks might have been useful, he explained that the community never had the opportunity to offer their own suggestions for the use of the funds. Who better to decide what their community needs than the people who live in the community? The organization was an outsider, and it not only failed to explain the appearance of the bike racks to the community, it failed to engage the community in determining the best way to use the funds in the first place.

The problem with many well-meaning nonprofit organizations, according to Russell, is that "you have all

Staff Writer Heather Moran drafts her article following an interview with Tyrone Russell. Students must complete all work during the Writing Wrongs program weekend. Bethlehem, Pa., Sept. 4, 2021. (Writing Wrongs/Shannon O'Connor)

1849 Harriet Tubman (1822-1913) escapes from slavery and travels north using the routes and safehouses of the Underground Railroad. She uses this geographical information to help dozens more escape slavery in the South.[21]

these folks pop up and they think they know everything, right? We've got our degrees, we got this, we know what you need. And rarely do they ask folks what's missing. Like, you're the experts in your own pain. Why are we acting like we know your pain when we haven't experienced it?"

In 2011 or 2012, Russell was part of the Water Fountain Project that included people of color from the community, advisers from Lehigh Valley corporations, and a local nonprofit, Community Action of the Lehigh Valley (CACLV). The Water Fountain Project was formed to identify racial wealth disparity in the community. Russell was clear to emphasize his insider role in the process and the need to approach the investigation without assumptions or bias.

"I don't want to say, 'finding the issues surrounding race in the Lehigh Valley,' because then we were out searching for answers. And when you're searching, you're going to find it. So, [the question was], is race a problem in the Lehigh Valley?"

The project found that there were racial disparities in education — only 4% of students taking the SAT were people of color. It also found that realtors were treating white and Black home buyers differently. The realtors were showing buyers with similar budgets homes in different areas based on their skin color.

In 1934, the Federal Housing Authority began the process that was eventually termed "redlining" — outlining and grading areas on city maps to indicate which areas were "safe" and which were "risky" for mortgage lenders. Black neighborhoods, outlined in red, received the lowest or riskiest grade. The consequences were far-reaching.

Home ownership is directly linked to generational wealth. Due to redlining, Black homeownership continues to be far lower than white homeownership. This translates to a similar inequality in wealth. Although redlining was outlawed in 1968 with the Fair Housing Act, which made it illegal to discriminate in the rental or sale of houses, the damage had already been done. Furthermore, as Russell found in his initial research with the Water Fountain Project, just because something is against the law doesn't mean it doesn't happen.

Russell doesn't have a specific life plan, but he does have one-, three-, and five-year goals and a desire to run his own business. He has had to find a balance between pursuing his dreams and contributing to his community.

After the Water Fountain Project was completed and recommendations had been made, Community Action of the Lehigh Valley recruited Russell to serve as the Coordinator of Racial and Ethnic Justice. Russell was

> **Due to redlining, Black homeownership continues to be far lower than white homeownership.**

working at Lehigh University and starting his company, Faces International, when Community Action of the Lehigh Valley approached him, but he agreed to give them two years of his time. While at CACLV, Russell helped to implement a program called Generation Next, which focused on helping first generation students and students of color with the college application process. Reflecting on his own experience, Russell realizes how much he benefited from the college sports recruitment process. "If I didn't have those folks coming to my door, I wouldn't really have known how to look for schools," he said. "My mom hadn't gone to college. Right? She didn't really understand the process."

Russell can relate to first-generation students and recognizes that their college challenges don't end with an acceptance letter. Getting into college is just the first of several hurdles first generation and low-income students face in their pursuit of a college degree. They often attend public schools that are underfunded and ill-equipped to provide adequate college advisement. Once on campus, first generation and low-income students of color often experience culture shock.

Russell recounts a visit to a predominantly white college to which, it seemed, all of the admitted students of color had been invited. The inclusivity the students felt during the visit was absent when the entire student body was present on campus, and the group of students who were culturally similar was diluted.

Since Russell was comfortable in new and diverse communities, his own challenges in college had less to do with his race. He found it harder to adjust to the lack of support he felt navigating life on campus as a first-generation college student. He recalls how he missed an important Colgate tradition — the incoming freshmen carry torches up a hill to signal their arrival at Colgate — simply because he was unaware that it was happening.

1851

Congress passes the first of several Indian Appropriations Acts. The 1851 Act allocates funds to create reservations which isolate Native Americans onto specified tracts of land and forcibly restricts their mobility. George Manypenny, Commissioner of Indian Affairs, believes that reservations are the only alternative to extermination.[22]

The tradition is completed when, as seniors, the students carry their torches down the hill. This is symbolic for Russell of his overall experience at Colgate. He didn't really become engaged at Colgate until midway through his time there and only then because he recognized that there were things the other students were doing that he wasn't, like connecting with the faculty.

Not all first-generation students and students of color are able to regain their footing the way Russell did. College drop-out rates are significantly higher for Black students than white students, according to the National Center for Education Statistics.

At the top of Russell's LinkedIn "Experience" section are his roles as the president of the Cleveland School of Cannabis and CEO of his management and development company, Faces International.

Cannabis is a hot emerging industry, and the Cleveland School of Cannabis helps its students learn about the sector so that they can pursue career opportunities. Russell is well aware of the history of marijuana in the United States and its connection to the mass incarceration of people of color, especially Black men. The legalization of a plant that is linked to those previously incarcerated or who continue to serve heavy-handed and discriminatory jail terms in connection with it contributes to the long history of the imbalance of power in our country. The fact that the white men who helped shape the policies that were used to justify those jail terms can now financially benefit from marijuana is hard to swallow.

Russell recognizes that, like most businesses, money is the key to the cannabis industry and that most people of color will be excluded. The Cleveland School of Cannabis' scholarship program helps individuals from marginalized communities, women, veterans, and people who have been harmed by the systemic racism that led to mass incarceration to gain access to the cannabis industry.

Faces International also plays a part in educating people. Russell's responsibilities as CEO include "a lot of diversity training, a lot of team development workshops, and a ton of business coaching, when it comes to building culture in [the] organization."

While the specifics of the companies are different, they share a similar goal of supporting the empowerment of others. The companies also have a symbiotic relationship. Russell provides training and development to the 57 staff members of the Cleveland School of Cannabis similar to what his Faces International clients receive. And his real-life engagement with CSC's workforce ensures that he is giving real world up-to-date training to his Faces International clients, rather than untested theories.

Russell recognizes that life is not static and he continues to learn and add new tools to his skillset. His business interests go well beyond the pursuit of profit. All of Russell's career pursuits are grounded in his social activism, pursuit of equality, and recognition of his gifts as a mentor. His leadership skills, which he has refined over a lifetime, grew out of his experiences at 11 different schools which inspired him to ask the questions: "Where do I fit? Where do I serve? How do I serve?"

Russell acknowledges the advantages he has had in his life and embraces the challenges too. His love for his mother, a nurse and first responder during the pandemic, is palpable as he talks about the photo of her hands that accompanied an article in the New York Times. The hands of Russell's mother, Valerie Wilson, set his lifepath in motion early in his life with her modeling of the importance of connecting with others.

"When I read that article, I just like, man — you don't have any idea what those hands really mean in terms of, like, giving me hugs, to disciplining me, to showing me the way — teaching me all this stuff," Russell said. "It's like, those hands for some are just these caring hands that they see in the hospital. But there's nothing better than reading an article and then seeing a picture of ... kind of your embrace."

Tyrone Russell's story is the story of a man who has made a life for himself despite systemic racism and who continues to actively fight against it. It is the story of a man who recognizes the gifts in his life, and instead of taking them for granted, uses them to support and encourage others. It is a story of a man whose mother showed him that a person can rise above adversity and care about others, even when their own life is challenging.

> **Tyrone Russell's story is not the story of a victim of racism.**

1857

In 1846, Dred Scott files a lawsuit arguing that because he had traveled to and lived in free states with his master, he was no longer a slave. The Missouri Supreme Court rules against Scott. In March 1857, the case reaches the Supreme Court of the United States, which rules that as an African American, Scott is not a citizen and is not entitled to his freedom. Among constitutional scholars, the Dred Scott case is considered to be the SCOTUS' worst decision in history.[23]

1861

The first full-scale battle of the Civil War, called the First Battle of Bull Run, takes place at Manassas, Virginia.[24]

MISTAKES AND MOVING ON

By Rohail Spear

Isaiah Johnson, Recording Engineer at NBH Studios and Blackroom Studios, volunteered to share his experiences at the Writing Wrongs program. Bethlehem, Pa., Sept. 4, 2021. (Writing Wrongs/Jennifer Berrios)

At age 18, Isaiah Johnson was arrested for attempted armed robbery after getting into a fight with a man who kicked him and his friend out of a fraternity house. Police officers witnessed the entire scene, surrounded Johnson, and took him to the police station. After his mother posted bail, Johnson was facing jail time. Unexpectedly, his basketball coaches and school teachers began writing letters in his defense, protesting the charge. "That's not this kid," they said. "He's [just] going through some stuff." Those letters advocating for Johnson's inherent goodness resulted in three years of probation instead of jail. Johnson admitted that he did a lot of "dumb stuff" in his teenage years, but throughout his entire life there were always people who saw past his mistakes to the potential within.

In middle school, Johnson was the cool kid. Basketball was "the only thing I was gifted at," he surmised. He was one of the best on the team. Bigger and taller than most of the other kids, Johnson admitted to often using his size to his advantage. He "wasn't a bully," but "nobody could … cross me or do anything wrong because I would just snap and people [would] be scared because I was bigger." Teachers would hold him back after class and ask why he took on this persona, why he "got to make fun of this dude … to look cool to these kids." He realizes now that almost everything he did back then was "for acceptance," for the "satisfaction of knowing that these people thought I was cool." Johnson felt pressure to maintain his status in the school and fill the large role of basketball star, and intimidation was his solution.

It was especially difficult for his teachers because they saw the good in him — they saw how he would, for example, introduce himself to the new kids and immediately befriend them. Indeed, Johnson remembers how people would come up to him and tell him stories of how

> "At twelve, I knew the way the system was set up."

1863

In the third year of the Civil War, President Lincoln issues the Emancipation Proclamation, which frees enslaved people in the southern states that had seceeded from the Union. The proclamation did not completely eliminate slavery — states that had not seceeded could continue enslavement — but the focus of the war is transformed. Both white abolitionists and enslaved people can now imagine a nation in which slavery does not exist.[25] In addition, the Union army can now enlist Black soldiers. More than 180,000 Black men join and fight in the Union army during the remainder of the war.[26]

he "was the one that introduced [them] to everybody"; he was the one who made them feel included.

The "dumb stuff" that Johnson referred to started in middle school when he repeatedly snuck his older friends into middle school dances. The first time he smuggled his friends in, he received detention. The second time, he was suspended. The third time was "the last straw" for the school: He was expelled. He reckons that the "crazy" stuff he was doing in class played a role in the school's decision to expel him.

Not all of Johnson's punishments were justified, however. He and his friends were playing hide-and-seek tag in a neighborhood after dark one night when, he said, "This dude calls the cops and says we're trying to break into his house." The police began patrolling the neighborhood, found Johnson, and told him that he fit the description of someone who had been breaking into houses near there. Johnson protested, but he insisted that the police "just flat out didn't believe me the whole time." Fortunately, he was taken back to his house, his mother was notified of what happened, the police let him go, and nothing further happened that night. Soon, however, Johnson received a letter in the mail telling him that the man who called the police was pressing charges against him and his friends. Apparently, the man had evidence that the back door knob was loose — Johnson believes that the man "went to the back door and ... loosened it because," he asserts, "we really, really didn't do it."

In court, Johnson's mother was "so scared" that she made him plead guilty. "We didn't have the money to get a lawyer; we didn't have the money to just go fight it," Johnson recalled. "He had a loose doorknob and it ... was just like, Wow. ... At twelve I knew the way the system was set up." Johnson was in seventh grade when this incident occurred. He admitted that that was "the scariest thing," scarier than anything that has happened to him since. He spent eighth grade on probation as a result of the incident.

After Johnson was expelled from middle school, he moved to the Pocono Mountains with his mother and stepfather — his parents divorced when he was two. He focused more on basketball in the Poconos and stayed out of trouble for the most part, but when he stole his stepfather's gun twice, his mother and stepfather argued to the point where they almost separated. He was forced to move back to Bethlehem with his father for his freshman year at high school. He then stole his father's car, twice. When his father found out about the second time, he kicked Johnson out of the house. Mystified, Johnson mused, "I'm doing stuff and I don't even know why I'm doing it," although looking back, he believes that it might have been for the adrenaline rush and instant gratification that risk-taking activities produce.

After Johnson's dad refused to allow him back in the house, Johnson's mother left her husband and moved to Bethlehem for him. For this, Johnson is "really appreciative. ... I just love her so much for always choosing me over anything," even the "love of her life."

Johnson graduated from high school in 2005. After high school, he attended Northampton Community College on a basketball scholarship, which he quickly lost after failing to put effort into the academic side of college. He moved in with his mom again, received a DUI for driving under the influence of marijuana, attended another college, received another DUI, and went to jail for three days. In those three days, a lot of people gave him advice and said things like "don't come back here." They, like his teachers, believed he was destined for more.

His mother eventually persuaded him to get a job, and Johnson started working at the Blue Grill House, a high-end restaurant, where he "just built the craziest bond with my boss, Caroline." Caroline was another person who believed in him: She helped him escape from a toxic relationship with his then-girlfriend. Unfortunately, his friend convinced him to quit the job with the promise that they could make more money selling insurance. The job quickly fell through, however, which was when Johnson started posting his beats on YouTube.

YouTube, marveled Johnson, "was like my break in producing." From YouTube, other producers noticed him; he started working with artists, and he landed a record deal. Johnson is now a full-time music producer and engineer. Recently, he has worked with Lil TJay, who has over six million followers on Instagram and has released three albums since 2019.

Johnson, 24, now lives with his girlfriend, his four-year old stepdaughter and his one-year old daughter. His future ambitions include creating a program where kids from all ages visit recording studios and record companies and learn how artists create and record music, how record deals are made, the advertising strategies of releasing albums, and the general workings of the music industry. He wants to enlighten children and teenagers of all the different paths they could follow in the music industry, whether business, marketing, performing, or writing. If he had something like that as a kid, he said, "There were so many things I wouldn't have had to second guess."

1863 — Harriet Tubman is the first African American woman to serve in the military, aiding Union commanders as a scout and spy during the Civil War. With Tubman's help, an African American regiment (the 2nd South Carolina Volunteer Infantry) frees more than 700 enslaved people in the raid at Combahee Ferry, South Carolina.[27]

1865 — Confederate General Robert E. Lee surrenders to Union General Ulysses S. Grant at Appomattox, Virginia, effectively ending the Civil War. The 13th Amendment is ratified eight months later (Dec. 1865), rendering slavery unconstitutional.[28,29]

STUCK BETWEEN TWO WORLDS

By Ben Hopper

The way our identities are crafted is a result of many complex characteristics. These properties that each of us possess — gender, sexuality, ethnicity, etc. — come together to define who we are as people. But these traits aren't always black and white in how they function, and as a result, can make defining one's identity much more difficult. This is something Dwight Holloway knows all too well.

Holloway is biracial: his mother is white and his father is Black. Growing up in Georgia, he felt he never fit completely into either group. As a result, he was often

> There wasn't anywhere he was safe from racism.

forced to play the parts of two different people, depending on whom he was with.

"You kind of have to shapeshift and mold your personality to kind of mix with whatever group you're with at the time," said Holloway. He didn't understand himself on an individual level; instead, he was defining himself based on whom he was around at the time.

When hanging out with people, Holloway did whatever the group wanted to do. This led him into situations where he wasn't comfortable. Participating in mud bogs and tractor pulls with his white friends put him in the same place as hateful racists. It was unspoken racism, present in the feeling of legions of hateful eyes locked on him. His childhood in Georgia was filled with incidents like these. There wasn't anywhere he was safe from racism.

Even sitting on the corner outside of his house, racism appeared in the form of a cop asking him for his ID card. Eleven-year-old Holloway, of course, didn't have an ID card; and upon hearing this, the officer followed up by asking him if he possessed any weapons or drugs. Holloway wasn't sitting on the corner with any ill intentions; it was simply a nice day and he loved to be outside. The cop responded by telling him to go inside. These weren't isolated incidents for young Holloway, who endured further racist harassment.

"Being chased, having things thrown at me, being called 'coon' in high school in the 2000s, having to switch partners for projects and school because the kids would be fine, but they're like, 'if you come to my house, my parents, they're not gonna let us work together,'" are incidents Holloway recounted.

Holloway no longer lives in Georgia. He now lives in Pennsylvania, which is a very different experience. Overall, he feels more comfortable in Pennsylvania; but

1865

Though the Emancipation Proclamation frees 3 million enslaved people in Confederate states, the news was slow to spread and enforce. African Americans in Galveston, Texas, remain enslaved for 2 ½ more years until June 19, when 2,000 Union troops arrive and officially inform them of their freedom. This day comes to be known as Juneteenth.[30]

In response to the 13th Amendment, southern white legislators pass black codes similar to the slave codes that denied freedmen their civil rights. Many of these repressive codes

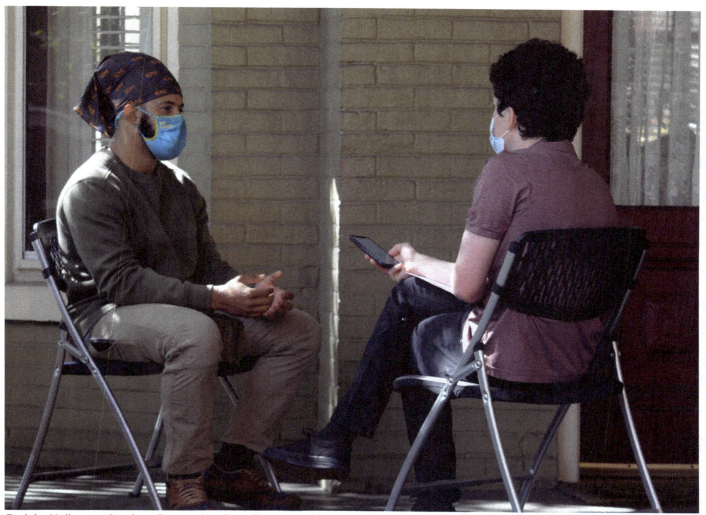

Dwight Holloway, Outdoor Recreation Coordinator at Afros in Nature, discusses his experiences with Staff Writer Ben Hopper. Bethlehem, Pa., Sept. 4, 2021. (Writing Wrongs/Jennifer Berrios)

still, when he goes to the more rural areas of the state there's an uncomfortable presence that he is aware of. Now he has a convenient system that helps him to determine if he'd feel comfortable stopping in a certain town: The more Trump flags there are in a given area, the less likely he is to stop there.

Holloway has learned from his negative experiences and now works to give back to the community. He joined the organization Afros in Nature looking to find likeminded people with whom to enjoy the outdoors. The mission of Afros in Nature is to provide Black, Indigenous, and people of color (BIPOC) the opportunity to connect with nature in order to improve mental health.

Now he's one of the core people in the organization. He's an outdoor recreation coordinator helping organize events, informing people about being safe outdoors, and teaching outdoor skills. The organization provides people with the opportunity to engage in activities, such as paddle boarding and bike riding, that would not be financially feasible for them otherwise. Holloway is adamant about the positive benefits nature brings to one's mental health.

"I mean, we came from nature, and now that we're so separated from it, it creates a lot of stress and doesn't give us places to reconnect and de-stress and kind of just forget about all the craziness of the world around us," Holloway affirmed.

Dwight Holloway's experiences didn't occur within a vacuum. They are struggles many other people of color go through. Holloway uses his love of the outdoors to help other people of color struggling with mental health. Here, Holloway is part of a team working to empower a community that has been routinely ignored.

Six Confederate veterans form the Ku Klux Klan (KKK) in Pulaski, Tennessee, supposedly as a social group. However, the elevated status of formerly enslaved people and other elements of Reconstruction are unsavory to many southerners, and additional branches of the KKK soon form with the aim of violently enforcing white supremacy in the American south. Congress passes the Enforcement Act and the Ku Klux Klan Act in 1870 with the purpose of ending voter intimidation and preventing the denial of equal justice under the law.[32]

BE YOUR AUTHENTIC SELF

Despite challenges, Allentown Councilwoman Ce-Ce Gerlach continues fighting for underrepresented communities

Ce-Ce Gerlach. Bethlehem, Pa., Sept. 4, 2021. (Writing Wrongs/Shannon O'Connor)

1868

The 14th Amendment is ratified, granting citizenship to everyone born or naturalized in the United States, thus giving Black Americans citizenship and reversing the Dred Scott decision. It also weakens the effect of black codes during Reconstruction of the South. The 14th Amendment guarantees due process and prohibits any former civil or military office holder who supported the Confederacy from again holding state or federal office.[33]

By Ebube Nwaeme and Cat Oriel

Growing up in the projects of Washington, D.C., Allentown Councilmember Ce-Ce Gerlach couldn't help but notice how race plays a role in society.

"I was raised by a white mom in a Black neighborhood," she said. "I knew we were poor. We wouldn't have Christmas if it wasn't for the Salvation Army. ... But seeing that there was this whole other world out there, [I thought], 'Why is it like that? Why is there such a divide?'"

Gerlach's upbringing, combined with Barack Obama's 2008 presidential campaign, jump-started her interest in impacting the community and fighting against the institutional barriers facing people of color. Gerlach followed the mantra, "Be the change you wish to see in the world," which pushed her to learn about politics by volunteering for the Obama campaign.

After attending Cedar Crest College in Allentown, where she has lived for the past 15 years, Gerlach accepted a job at the Boys and Girls Club, an organization that impacted her life as a child, and joined the Allentown School District (ASD) board. She quickly realized the ASD leadership did not reflect the diverse population they represented, which has led to systemic injustices within the community.

"Racism is alive and well in the Lehigh Valley," she said. "A lot of people don't view kids of color, and especially poor kids of color, as valuable. I've heard people within the institutions call our kids in Allentown the most derogatory names like 'animals' and 'untrained.'"

According to the Lehigh Valley Planning Commission, white residents are two times more likely to live in a high opportunity area and three times more likely to graduate from high school than non-white people. Although Gerlach was aware of these disparities, especially within the leadership, she didn't speak up immediately.

"I wanted to fit in. I wanted them to like me. I wanted to be accepted. I wanted to get invited to those little wine and cheese dinners," she said. This was Gerlach's thought process when she first got into the commission in about 2015. She switched her perspective to "I'm not them. I'll never be them. I don't want to be like them. They are the problem."

She decided to run for city council when she realized a lot of the work she was trying to do on the school board was more community-based and an attempt to empower families. Gerlach, who identifies as Black but also has white heritage, acknowledges how her racial ambiguity benefited her during the campaigning process, allowing her to win a nomination in both the Republican and Democratic primaries. Gerlach understands this when she knocks on people's doors and they don't know what race she is.

"They don't know how to be racist towards me," she says. "They don't know what stereotypes to give me. They're more willing sometimes to actually listen to what you're saying versus pigeon-holing you into what race you are. ... [But] at the end of the day, you're a person of color."

Throughout her time on the council, she has focused on a myriad of issues including reducing homelessness. Her first piece of legislation led to the formation of the Allentown Commission on Homelessness. This was fostered by the statistics that showed more than a thousand students were experiencing homelessness within the Allentown School District. Through her efforts, the commission's yearly budget has increased to include $100,000 being allocated toward homelessness. She also helped the city receive $57 million from the American Rescue Plan to build a year-round shelter.

Additionally, she has worked to increase jobs in the Allentown area. According to Gerlach, 80 percent of jobs located in Allentown are held by non-residents. Her new legislation, the First Source Ordinance, would require any business to hire a certain number of local residents.

She highlighted criminal justice reform as another larger passion. Instead of mass incarceration, she believes in promoting rehabilitation and mental health services, ending cash bail, and allocating resources and responsibilities away from the police force.

"Racism is alive and well in the Lehigh Valley."

1870

The 15th Amendment is ratified, stating that the right to vote will not be abridged based on race, creed, color, or national origin, thus giving Black men the right to vote in America. Many southern states enact laws to thwart this Amendment, such as literacy tests and "grandfather clauses" that deny the right to vote to anyone whose ancestors had not voted in the 1960s.[34]

Despite her accomplishments, Gerlach has faced challenges as well. Since she is not "the typical person that holds office," she has to work "twenty times as hard" as most of her white male counterparts to gain respect. Gerlach is forced to make sure she's on top of her game when it comes to her physical appearance, dress, and speech.

Gerlach was inspired to run for Allentown mayor in 2021 to be able to implement all the laws she created during her time on the council. However, Gerlach was charged with child endangerment during her campaign, a situation currently in litigation.

When asked if racial discrimination could potentially play a role in the allegations during the campaign and subsequent charges made against her, she said: "It's played a role in everything else. So one could make the argument that it's playing a role with my current situation. It makes sense from the establishment point of view."

Although she was warned not to talk about racial issues when she first joined office in 2015, she realized she could no longer stay silent — much to the dismay of her colleagues. In 2020, she was called to resign by fellow council members for attending Black Lives Matter protests. This censure encouraged Gerlach to continue advocating even though she believed others in the council did not want her to succeed.

"I want to flip the systems upside down," she said. "If you are someone who is benefiting from the systems the way they currently are, then it is in your best interest to make sure that I do not get to a position where I can flip the system upside down."

The trial is forthcoming, but Gerlach claims the whole story will soon come out. She notes that regardless of the outcome and where the future takes her, she is determined to continue fighting for underrepresented communities she is invested in.

"I want to be on a body of people that is making laws and changing laws," she said. "I don't want to be at home screaming at my TV; I want to be the person that is being screamed at on TV."

Regardless of the pushback she has faced for being outspoken, standing up for what she believes in has left her "soul at ease." Gerlach's advice for the upcoming generation of people of color trying to gain power and influence, especially in the Lehigh Valley, is that it's "okay to have people hate you and it's okay to be uncomfortable."

"People should be mad that you are at that table — because we're at tables to destruct," she said. "Just be your authentic self. You don't have to look like them or talk like them. Do you."

Allentown Councilwoman Ce-Ce Gerlach. Bethlehem, Pa., Sept. 4, 2021. (Writing Wrongs/Jennifer Berrios)

Editor's note: *At a hearing in Lehigh County Court on March 30, 2022, prosecutors withdrew the child endangerment count against Gerlach. On the count of failure to report or refer (by a mandated reporter), Gerlach was accepted into the accelerated rehabilitation disposition (ARD) program for first-time offenders. Upon completion of the 24-month program, her arrest record will be expunged.*

NIGERIAN HISTORY: A TOOL FOR RACIAL JUSTICE

By Milena Berestko

Her energy entered the room before she did. Speaking slowly, carefully weighing each word is characteristic of Chekwube Okunowo, who is one of the staff writers for the 2021 Writing Wrongs program. She is a sophomore at Drew University in New Jersey studying International Relations with minors in Economics and Law and Justice in Society. Okunowo was born in Boston and then moved back to her parents' homeland, Nigeria, where she lived for 17 years. She recently returned to the United States to pursue her college education. Her former life in Nigeria was drastically different from the one she now leads in the U.S. Here, she is more often perceived by her race: "Growing up in Nigeria, I did not experience the microaggressions that people experience in the U.S. I grew up around people who look like me, who are all Black. At the same time, while I lived in Nigeria, there was this white supremacy you noticed."

Racism takes on many shapes and forms. In Nigeria, it hides in conversations, in acts of kindness directed at light-skinned residents, in neglected history. "Whenever a white family would move to the area and their children would move to the school, all eyes would be on the children because they were white. Automatically those kids would be treated better than the rest of us," Okunowo shared. White people in Nigeria are addressed with respect reminiscent of the respect the slave masters received in the past. "If they [white people] are coming to Nigeria, then they are probably working for the oil industry when Nigerians are their drivers, their maids in the house," Okunowo said. "There was always this kind of imbalance in Nigeria." The power scale is unbalanced. Native Nigerians are under the jurisdiction of white visitors/newcomers, and the disparity doesn't end there.

White parents also had better relationships and greater allowances with school teachers. When resources are scarce, race determines who wins the zero-sum game. Whites always get more. Okunowo stated, "Teachers don't have enough textbooks, notebooks, teaching materials to teach the students. When you have people who are thinking about what they are going to eat the next day, students and teachers alike, people are not going to teach or learn effectively." One must satisfy their hunger before they can proceed to address higher-order needs. Education is transformative and empowering, but it requires energy that students did not have.

Okunowo believes that knowledge of history would reduce the worshiping of white men in Africa. She shared, "There are still many older people in Nigeria who literally bow down to the white men and treat fellow Nigerians as though they are less than the white men." However, learning is easier said than done. Access to history proves to be a rarity. Okunowo stated matter-of-factly, "There were no history classes in middle school. You learn some basic history of Nigeria in elementary school, but it was not expanded. When did we receive independence in Nigeria? In 1960. But who did we gain independence from? How did our culture change? Why is Western culture so glorified in our society? All these things, we didn't learn." History classes in Nigeria were always optional. Ancestral wisdom is disappearing as schools fail to teach it, and families have other matters to worry about. "Grandparents told stories of the past or civil

> "There are still many older people in Nigeria who literally bow down to the white men and treat fellow Nigerians as though they are less than the white men."

1887

President Grover Cleveland signs the Dawes Act into law, which divides communally owned Reservation lands into privately owned plots. After allotting specific acres of reservation land to individual Native Americans (to be held in trust for 25 years), the government then purchases the remaining 86 million acres and makes them available to white settlers. The Dawes Act is another attempt to force assimilation by subverting the Native American culture of tribal organization and encouraging them to become farmers.[36]

Staff Writer Chekwubechi Okunowo (left) talks about her own experiences with racism with Staff Writer Milena Berestko. Bethlehem, Pa., Sept. 5, 2021. (Writing Wrongs/Jennifer Berrios)

war, but it wasn't a big thing," she said. "In my family, history wasn't the primary focus. Most people are just trying to survive, so the focus is not on the history."

Other obstacles to learning about Nigerian history are geographic differences and divisions. "The North is predominantly Muslim, so most of the schools in the North were learning the Islamic culture," Okunowo said. "The focus was not on ancestry or how some of the fellow Nigerians sold other Nigerians into slavery. It was mostly on religion. Conversations in the family revolve around religion and survival: How to be successful, how to not get scammed, but nothing of the past."

Religious doctrines during the colonial era were used to subordinate Nigerians. "The majority of Muslim people believed that whatever happened was God's will, and so they were more submissive to the colonial masters," Okunowo said. "Because of that, masters loved and appreciated them more." She analyzed the history and thus is able to point out the remnants of slavery and the mannerisms of the enslaved: unearned respect given to the whites. She is able to call out the practices that prevail yet should have crumbled with Nigerian independence in 1960.

"History helped me remove the supremacy of the white man that society ingrained in my mind," she said. "Learning history, understanding the history of the enslavement of the African people, understanding being Black, white, understanding the history of suffering of the Black people — it helped me wipe away the glory for the white man." Okunowo used history as a way to regain her power while other Nigerians chose to protest.

"Hundreds of Black people protesting on the streets for their lives to matter can never go unnoticed," she said. The protest was a social awakening for many. "The movement woke people up to social justice issues. Similar things were happening to the End SARS Movement. Black Lives Matter (BLM) was an inspiration for them [Nigerian protesters]." Nigerians were not only protesting for their rights at home but also for their families in the U.S. Okunowo is hopeful to see a shift in narrative: "History could be forgotten and left out from the picture, but awareness is coming back due to the Black Lives Matter Movement." It must take the whole village to eradicate racism, especially when "the older generations with white supremacist views train younger generations on how to follow these views." Internalized racism gets passed on. It needs to be seen, acknowledged, unlearned, and then eradicated to reintroduce equity.

Okunowo is advocating for equity of happiness through abolishing white supremacy. "I am big on happiness and love and loving one another as we love ourselves, and [people] getting the happiness they deserve. Not the happiness they think they deserve, but the happiness they actually deserve. I think that [happiness] happens when everyone is treated with equity," she asserted. Equity means access to the records of the past; it means equal treatment and enjoying resources one needs (using white people's metric of need). It means access to quality education and having the ability to share one's story to make history.

In response to the U.S. Government's broken treaties and the hardships of reservation life, Native Americans across the western plains states begin practicing a spiritual ritual called the Ghost Dance. The government views the dances as hostile and dispatches the Army to several Lakota reservations to stop them; Sioux holy man Chief Sitting Bull (1831–1890) is killed during one confrontation. At Wounded Knee Creek, South Dakota, the Army fires upon a group of Miniconjou Lakota with Hotchkiss guns after most had relinquished their weapons. An estimated 150–300 unarmed Lakota, including women and children, are massacred.[37]

DON'T QUIT. KEEP GOING.

By Luka Marjanovic

"You have a blank canvas. You're the paintbrush, so you have to create your own story," said Matthew Riddick, a 33-year-old resident of eastern Pennsylvania. Riddick is a pharmaceutical executive by day and an owner of a healthcare insurance consulting company focusing on Black and Brown communities by night.

He earned his bachelor's degree in business administration from Delaware Valley University in Doylestown, Pennsylvania, as well as earning his Juris Doctor (law degree) from Villanova University in Philadelphia. He is currently enrolled in an online Master of Business Administration (MBA) program at Longwood University and recently married. Riddick began his interview talking about his four year-old dog Trinity, demonstrating how well he manages to balance his aspirations and successes with simple pleasures of life.

During Riddick's undergraduate years, he worked in a family-owned shoe store. After graduating, his mom told him to find a real job, "one he can actually get fired from." Upon his asking how to do this, she told young Matthew: "Well, start with the A's. Just go online and start with the A's." This search led to his first job at Allstate, which in turn led to other opportunities, which in turn led to founding his own consulting company in 2019.

When explaining the vision for his company, Riddick cites the following event that led to its creation: "I was speaking to my cousin and she picked her life insurance and health insurance at random, because she picked out of fear, and she was overly insured, and it was costing her a lot of money." After hearing this litany of obstacles his cousin faced, Riddick felt a need to find a solution: "I had a revelation, like, I wonder how many people do that. Yeah, I find out a lot of people take that route because they do not understand health insurance; they do not understand the market. They think, the bigger the better."

Not only did this discussion lead to the founding of a successful Black-owned business, but it also gave Riddick an opportunity to exercise his biggest passion, which is education — that is, educating others.

When asked where his love for education comes from, he answered, "Because I just realized how many people are uneducated about the healthcare system, and they don't understand the laws. They don't understand what they're selecting. They don't understand why it costs as much as it does. They don't understand the different public policy behind it."

1896

Homer Plessy and a group of New Orleans citizens challenge Louisiana's "Separate Car Act," which states that African Americans must use separate railway cars from white travelers. The Louisiana Supreme Court decision in Plessy v. Ferguson upholds racial segregation, declaring "separate but equal" Jim Crow laws legal and constitutional.[38]

> "I truly believe, in every aspect, the more educated we are and the more informed we are, the better decisions we can make."

This inspired him to create something that would inspire others, educate others, and create meaningful change in the Black and Brown communities of this area. Education continues to be his driving force, and he reiterates that with every answer he gives: "So, I truly believe, in every aspect, the more educated we are and the more informed we are, the better decisions we can make."

Riddick's business works on a sliding economic scale, adaptable to whether the customer is an individual or a family and dependent on their economic status. This also leads to consulting pro bono, which was the case with a particular family that was in a difficult financial situation. "In this case I made a decision to just consult pro bono. And I was able to assist this family to get a very bottom line, a very cost-efficient package for their family," Riddick said. "I was able to educate them further for future transactions." Not only that, but that family continued using Riddick's services because of how comfortable they felt. Riddick saves lives, saves finances, and provides comfort while educating at every chance he gets.

Passion is very important to Riddick's way of living, and he considers every successful professional and personal endeavor as an art form. "I believe that when you're passionate about something or that you've done something for so long and you trained your mind to do it, you know it's an art form," he said. "It's your craft. I believe everyone should try and perfect, or come close to perfection, whatever their craft is."

Riddick has spent the last ten years perfecting his craft, and he will continue doing so, in his own way, carving his own path in a world that is filled with hurdles. "Everybody does it in different ways, and they take different avenues to get to that finish line, but it's your canvas. Just use that as your paintbrush to create your masterpiece, however you want to do it. And it's going to be a masterpiece because it's your story," he said. "So that's why I say for me, it's an art form. My business, marriage, my life was all a blank canvas, and I'm the one holding the paintbrush and creating my story. You know you are forming and perfecting your life. So even with my consulting firm, it's an art form because I'm not doing it the same way that my counterpart is doing it." Everything seems more magical through Riddick's viewpoint and words, even day-to-day life and occurrences within it.

The fact that he was diagnosed with Crohn's disease in November of 2020 makes everything Riddick does for the education of the Black and Brown communities regarding healthcare even more significant. Riddick explains that Crohn's disease is "a full body disease that can affect your eyesight; it can affect your joints in terms of pains and discomfort; and obviously, of course, it affects your small intestine. It makes you more immobile and causes things like colon cancer and intestinal cancer." Still, this did not stop him from continuing his fight to educate the Black and Brown community about healthcare opportunities. He says that he uses his disease as a connecting bridge with people who face similar issues and weekly $30,000 bills if they are not properly insured.

Riddick offered one final piece of advice for anybody trying to find their place in our unpredictable world: "Just don't quit. Just keep going, because the prize is so much greater because you conquered that mountain."

1899

The Philippine-American war begins after the U.S. acquires the islands from Spain and refuses to annex the country. The racial climate of the U.S. dominates its relations with Filipinos, whom many in power view as inferior. This war poses a dilemma of conscience for African American men in the military, who are viewed similarly by their American colleagues. Filipino nationalists target African Americans in their media campaigns for independence, pointing out that the U.S. is only using them to achieve their goals of colonization. Over 200,000 Filipino civilians are

Matthew Riddick, Founder and Operator of The Riddick Foundation, speaks to the Writing Wrongs group about inequities in health care. Bethlehem, Pa., Sept. 5, 2021. (Writing Wrongs/Alliana Myers)

1909

The National Association for the Advancement of Colored People (NAACP) is formed "to work for the abolition of segregation and discrimination in housing, education, employment, voting, and transportation; to oppose racism; and to ensure African Americans their constitutional rights." Founding members include W.E.B. DuBois, Ida B. Wells Barnett, and Mary White Ovington. The organization publishes "The Crisis" magazine.[40]

A PATH OF PERSEVERANCE AND PASSION

By Ben Hopper

Things were never easy for Hayden Craddolph. During his childhood, he endured a lot of bullying, much of it racially motivated. Peers insulted him for being biracial, calling him names like "Oreo cookie." Even outside of school, he had to deal with racism. He lived next to Ku Klux Klan members growing up, who repeatedly put racist and threatening stickers on his family's car — stickers that read "Die," sometimes with a racial slur attached. Though some people would be slowed down by this, Craddolph found himself motivated. The bullying and racism were an incentive, fueling him to work harder.

In gym class, during a two-hand touch football game, Craddolph excelled. His speed was quickly noticed by his classmates. Classmates still bullied him with racist attacks, but now there was also a group of classmates that wanted him on their team during sports. In athletics, he found himself accepted by his peers. However, he is quick to dispel the idea of athletics being a one-size-fits-all situation where it is the key to stopping every individual's bullying problem. "But I felt that at least it worked for me," Craddolph said. "I had a passion for watching sports on TV when I was a child. So again, it was a form of escapism. And then when I was bullied, I leveraged that as a way to really, quite frankly, stop the bullying."

Passion was the driving force during Craddolph's childhood that helped him overcome the racist bullying he faced. That passion, that drive to continue forward, has never dissipated from Craddolph's life or his attitude towards it. Challenges have continued to present themselves, but he has persevered no matter the struggle he faces. More recently, it has been his passion for film that's led him to become who he is today. Passion is what made him completely change his career path, leaving a successful job on Wall Street to go back to school to pursue his passion for film.

Speaking to the Writing Wrongs staff, Craddolph's every word was articulated with the passion, wisdom, and experience he has accumulated through the years. Craddolph knows the importance of education, which was at the heart of his speech. He addressed education as an opportunity for empowerment. The fact that

Hayden Craddolph (center). Bethlehem, Pa., Sept. 5, 2021. (Writing Wrongs/Alliana Myers)

1916

African Americans in the south face lack of job opportunities and constant struggle against oppressive Jim Crow laws. Through 1970, six million Black people move from the rural south to northern and western cities during the Great Migration, initiating Black arts and cultural movements such as the Harlem Renaissance in New York City.[41]

Hayden Craddolph (center), Founder of Haydenfilms LLC and Haydenfilms Film Institute, participates in a panel of Lehigh Valley leaders speaking to the Writing Wrongs group. Bethlehem, Pa., Sept. 5, 2021. (Writing Wrongs/Shannon O'Connor)

not everyone is allotted this opportunity is something Craddolph is cognizant of. He would not be here if it were not for education, and he urges people to seek it as well. He spoke about the need to find the will and motivation to keep going through education in order to pursue one's passion.

Although the challenges, gambles and risks were plentiful throughout Craddolph's journey, his decision to leave his old life in the corporate sphere to become a full-time student was also a gamble. There weren't any guarantees it would pay off. A lot of other people in his position would not have made the same choice he did; fear of the unknown would have prevented them from making that leap. There were two major factors that led him to go back to school — the pressure of his Wall Street job and the travel his work required. Commuting from Bethlehem to New York City, along with the stressful work environment, was tearing apart his work-life balance. It was after being trapped in a bus for twelve hours in the midst of a snowstorm when he really meditated on whether this job was what he really wanted. His family had always stressed the importance of education. With that in mind, and being unhappy with his job, he decided to go back to school. It was a major risk and he sacrificed a lot.

Another risk he took was founding his own online film festival. It started with pitching his idea for a film at Kutztown University's Small Business Development Center. He pitched his film to a "fifty-year-old white guy" who had no faith in Craddolph's ability to succeed. It was then that he thought to take the $10,000 he would have used to create his own film and instead use it to create an online film festival showcasing other people's films. He founded Haydenfilms LLC in 2001. While creating a film and creating an online film festival are both risky ventures, creating one's own online film festival is much less common; and thus, success in this venture becomes less

1921

Because of a misunderstanding of what happened in an elevator between Dick Rowland, a Black man, and Sarah Page, a white woman, white residents of Tulsa, Oklahoma loot, riot, and burn down the thriving Greenwood district known as Black Wall Street.[42] Approximately 300 people die and over $1.4 million in property claims are filed against the city, most of which are denied. Greenwood is completely destroyed and many of the nearly 11,000 Black residents of Tulsa are left homeless.[43]

Alexis Jacquet, Staff Social Media Manager, records footage of the speakers' panel to post on Writing Wrongs' social media channels. Bethlehem, Pa., Sept. 5, 2021. (Writing Wrongs/Alliana Myers)

likely. Craddolph was routinely taking these risky leaps and having them pay off. He feels this risk worked out for him due to his putting the community first. "If you put the community first, if you follow your bliss, you follow your passion, the money and all that other stuff will come," he said. "That's how I felt about the online film festival. And supporting filmmakers for those four years opened up this whole new world that has now been able to generate revenues and things of that nature."

Another aspect of Craddolph's success can certainly be attributed to his insistence that the filmmaker he is working with be more important than himself. This happens when the ego is put aside and art is given more importance. Craddolph reasserted this idea by retelling a story from the making of the movie "Jaws." During the opening sequence, director Steven Spielberg realized the shark didn't work. That opening scene is one of the most iconic scenes in film history, hugely because of how they needed to tell the story in a completely different artistic way. If ego was in play and Spielberg refused to proceed without a working shark, the scene would not be as famous as it is. "If they were thinking about the ego thing — 'I'm not making this film until the shark works. I can't believe you're doing this to me, don't you know who I am, blah, blah, blah' — and that was Steven Spielberg's mindset, the masterpiece would have never been made," Craddolph explained. "But he put the art before his own ego. And that's how I feel about the festival as well."

Financial literacy has been imperative for his success; as such, Craddolph has a deep passion for it. He explains how check cashing businesses are so prominent in urban environments. Whenever someone uses them, they pay around $17 in fees. This is especially a problem for people living paycheck to paycheck. It is much more financially efficient to pay a singular monthly bank fee when their balance is below a certain amount than paying multiple fees per month. He feels financial literacy is not focused upon enough, and teaching it should be mandatory in school. Growing up, just like his parents before him, he did not learn financial literacy. It was not until later in life that he developed financial knowledge and skills.

It is quite apparent how this system disproportionately impacts people of color. Craddolph describes how these systems take advantage of those lacking financial literacy. "Usually you see it in urban communities, right? Check cashing places ... Everything is taking their money faster than they can replenish their money," Craddolph explained. This leaves the question of whether such a complicated, entangled, old, and broken system is able to be untangled and fixed. Craddolph feels the corporate greed present in the system prevents it from being changed. "How do you fix that? You're not going to fix it from the banking side," he said. "They're actually adding those fees as a way of preying on ... uneducated or non-financially literate [people]." Because of the predatory nature of this system, financial literacy is necessary to avoid being taken advantage of.

Many factors led Hayden Craddolph to be successful. He believed in the power of education and was willing to take the risk of leaving his high-paying job to attend college. He took a gamble by deciding to form his own online film festival rather than produce his own film. He overcame the racist bullying and harassment that characterized his childhood, using it as inspiration that made him work harder. He never let anything slow him down; no challenges were ever enough to stop him from pursuing his passion. He has persevered through it all, his passion for film lighting the way through the dark.

1923

Bhagat Singh Thind, an Indian Sikh man, comes to Portland, Oregon in 1912 to pursue an education. He serves in the latter part of WWII and is honorably discharged. Seeking U.S. citizenship, Thind challenges the Naturalization Act of 1790, which states that only "free white persons" could become citizens. Thind's lawyers argue that he is white based on ethnologic research that claimes the white race includes Caucasian peoples of northern India. The Supreme Court does not agree, and denies Thind citizenship because he is "Hindoo" and therefore can never be white.[44]

MURDER, MINISTRY, AND MISDIAGNOSIS:

The Story of Veronica James

By Cat Oriel

When Veronica James' children reached middle school, she began sitting them down around the dinner table to have The Talk: How to navigate living in America as a Black person. Like many Black parents, James' biggest concern for her children was violence and harassment inflicted by law enforcement. Although they are now adults, she still continues to inform her kids about what to do when pulled over by a police officer.

Her constant advice paid off when Olric, one of her four sons, was pulled over by a cop in high school. After Olric handed over his identification and paperwork, the policeman expressed shock that he was not already in the system. This experience reaffirmed James' warning that police officers generally approach Black men with stereotypes and biases. However, she was ultimately grateful that her son handled the situation with care and defied the cop's pre-existing expectations. "Be proud of yourself," she said to her son, "because they don't expect anything good out of a young Black man."

James, a resident of the Lehigh Valley for 33 years, has experienced many instances of racism within the area. When she first arrived in Bethlehem from Guyana, she immediately experienced difficulties when attempting to find work. She applied for many jobs only to keep getting rejected. Eventually, she volunteered 1,000 hours until she got a position in a hospital working in the kitchen while also attending school. "Bethlehem is horrible when it comes to prejudice," she said.

Despite the biases James has experienced within the greater area, for her, coming back every week to the St. John AME Church has helped her overcome many struggles. Her grandmother was a "proud" member who continued to bring James to church each week, which has led the congregation to become vital to the family. "There have been so many challenges in my life, that if I didn't believe and have that faith in God, I would not have been able to survive a lot of things that I've encountered," James said.

Although her strict parenting style has mostly kept her children out of trouble, in March 2021, her son Ukee was found dead while on a trip to Ethiopia. While the official cause of death was ruled a suicide, James believes her son was murdered. "I tried to instill in them to believe and trust God, always pray and do things that they're supposed to do," she said. "I still ended up losing one of my sons and that was really devastating to me."

Her faith in God and the supportive church community helped James get through the grieving process. Although Ukee's memorial was not held at St. John AME due to COVID-19 concerns, members from

1924 Congress signs the Indian Citizenship Act into law, granting citizenship to those Indigenous Americans who did not receive it through the Dawes Act. Voting rights, however, are governed by state law and some states bar Native Americans from voting until 1957.[45]

St. John AME Zion Church, Bethlehem, Pa., Sept. 5, 2021. (Writing Wrongs/Jennifer Berrios)

the church and pastors still showed up to support her. "It's because I trust and believe in God that gives me the strength to continue living," she said. "I had family constantly come in and out those first few days. I got through because I had people around comforting me." As a single mother, James has one piece of advice for those in a similar situation: "Keep your children close. Talk to them all the time. Keep them in the faith. Let them learn and believe that they can trust somebody," she said. "Keep them informed all the time about what's going on [in the news]. Just talk to your children."

Although James has faced challenges raising her children, she has also encountered her own personal physical struggles due to what she sees as racial discrimination by health care providers. In 2019, James was diagnosed with breast cancer but believes the diagnosis was a mistake. "My new genetic tests show that it was negative for cancer," she said. "When I was doing all the treatments, I felt like I was being violated because I had no symptoms of all these women who were diagnosed with triple negative breast cancer. The way that I was treated, it was like they were hiding something."

The doctors removed her lymph nodes, which showed no sign of cancer, but still decided to remove her breast tissue. However, when she talked to her white female surgeon about the pain she was experiencing after her breast reconstruction, the doctor dismissed James and told her she was fine. A plastic surgeon in Washington, D.C., confirmed James' belief that the implants were too big and needed to be fixed. However, that doctor's referral, a physician in Philadelphia, ultimately dismissed the recommendation. "[The doctor] looked at me and she told me, 'I don't see anything wrong. It's only your nipples; you have good cleavage.' I said, 'No, I was misdiagnosed.' She gave me my papers, threw them on the desk, walked out of the room, and left me sitting right there," James said.

The side effects worsened and James experienced additional damages to her body, such as fractures in both feet and her toenails and fingernails falling off. Despite getting a port painfully inserted for chemotherapy, she ultimately decided to stop treatments against her family doctor's wishes. James has contacted twelve lawyers to see if they can help her file a malpractice suit. All of them turned her down, which James believes is because attorneys are afraid to go up against a big institution like a large regional hospital.

The excruciating pain continues to spread throughout her body and affects her ability to continue working a physically demanding job. Because she could no longer work at the job she had when she was diagnosed, she didn't have insurance. She has since regained coverage and is training for a less strenuous position. The implants have also affected her ability to get a good night's sleep.

While James does not have any answers as to next steps in resolving her medical issues, she is certain about one thing: "Young Black women are being abused by the healthcare system and our young Black men are being abused by the cops."

Editor's Note: Veronica James died in June 2023.

1929

Charles Curtis (1860–1936) becomes the first Native American Vice President, serving in President Herbert Hoover's administration. He is the only multiracial person to hold this title until Kamala Harris' inauguration in 2021. Curtis also serves in the House of Representatives from 1892 to 1907. During this time, he sponsors the Curtis Act, an amendment to the Dawes Act that is detrimental to Native Americans. To this day, VP Curtis remains the highest ranking government official of Indigenous descent. [46]

RENEWED PERSPECTIVE

By Jesse Marsh and Ebube Nwaeme

When Honey Bee decided to emigrate from Jamaica to the United States for economic opportunity, she had no idea what to expect. Growing up in an environment where the melting pot of people treated others with love and respect, it was a shock to her how different America was.

"When I came here, I was located in Long Island, New York, and I saw a lot of differences in how [Americans] treat Black people from Caucasians, and unfortunately, it was to my surprise," she said.

It took Bee a while to get adapted. With young children and no one to guide her, she made a tough decision to send her kids to live with her mother back in Jamaica while she built a solid foundation in the U.S. for their eventual return.

Once she figured out her situation, it was time to bring her children back. With that decision, she faced a monumental task of teaching them how to navigate the United States as Black people. When her kids left for Jamaica, they were so young and had no idea what racism was. Now she had to give The Talk, a conversation every Black parent in America must have with their children. Bee said, "I told my children they must respect each and everyone, regardless of their background. Whether they're Asian, American, whoever they are, each and every individual must be respected."

Due to the bouts of racism she observed in New York, combined with the rise in crime, Bee knew she needed to leave the state to put her kids in a better position to succeed. As much as she wanted to get them away from racism, she knew that was impossible in America. She took a chance with somewhere that was safer and had a better education system, landing in Bethlehem, Pennsylvania. "My main interest was getting them a proper education and not too much violence. I realized and understood that no matter where you go, there's going to be racism there," she recalled.

Working in law enforcement her entire life in Jamaica took a toll on Bee, so she opted for a career change. She combined her love for cooking and the Caribbean and opened a restaurant, saying, "As a child, I always said, I choose two ways: being in the medical field or opening a restaurant. I love cooking. Cooking is my passion."

Her career change was not smooth sailing at the beginning. Business was doing well, but her landlord did

> "We also as Black people need to start treating ourselves better and uplifting and respecting each other. If you see one [Black person] going up, raise that one up instead of pulling that one down. It's got to start with us."

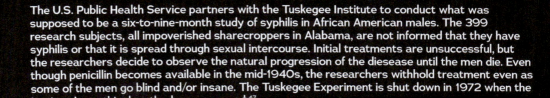

The U.S. Public Health Service partners with the Tuskegee Institute to conduct what was supposed to be a six-to-nine-month study of syphilis in African American males. The 399 research subjects, all impoverished sharecroppers in Alabama, are not informed that they have syphilis or that it is spread through sexual intercourse. Initial treatments are unsuccessful, but the researchers decide to observe the natural progression of the diesease until the men die. Even though penicillin becomes available in the mid-1940s, the researchers withhold treatment even as some of the men go blind and/or insane. The Tuskegee Experiment is shut down in 1972 when the not like that. According to Bee, once he saw she was doing well, he decided to raise the rent. He also prohibited her from expanding her offerings within her restaurant. She felt he wanted to do everything in his power to prevent her from succeeding. "He had a blue car, a blue SUV, and he came and sat in front of [the restaurant] every day. He'd tell me how many customers I had for the day," Bee remembers.

Once Bee raised an issue with his behavior, and he proceeded to pelt her with the most dehumanizing word a Black person can hear. "He called me a n-----," she emotionally recollected.

A whirlwind of thoughts went through Bee's head as she heard the word come from her landlord's mouth. She knew that what he said more than crossed the line, and she had every right to react strongly. Although she really wanted to, thinking long-term, she knew she had to keep cool, calm, and collected. "Oh God, I lost it for a second. I had to compose myself [in order] not to be behind bars," Bee said.

The incident forced Bee to close her business. Though it was an unfair situation, she did not allow the experience to tear her down. Instead, she took time to regroup and put a substantial amount of thought into her next move. Bee used the encounter with her former landlord for growth. She found a landlord in a neighboring town with whom she meshed well, and five years ago, became the first and currently only Black business owner in the area.

Already proving she was a successful businesswoman at her previous location, her restaurant instantly became a hit in its new abode. She's received numerous accolades throughout her five years and has felt extreme love and support from everyone in the predominantly white community. "In the community where I have my business, I am highly accepted, appreciated and I take it as an honor," Bee proclaimed.

As a result of her newfound positive experiences as a businesswoman, she has high hopes for the future of race relations in the Lehigh Valley area. When asked about the steps needed to achieve equality in the area, she says it starts within the black community.

"We also as Black people need to start treating ourselves better and uplifting and respecting each other. ... If you see one [Black person] going up, raise that one up instead of pulling that one down. It's gotta start with us."

Looking at the acceptance and support the community gives to Honey Bee and her establishment, it shows all people can co-exist with love and care, regardless of the color of their skin. From Bee's experience, Black people can see that no matter what racist incidents one encounters, they can come out on the winning side. Bee's story serves as encouragement for young Black individuals looking to start a business in the Lehigh Valley. It shows that if they have the proper support, the sky is the limit.

Writing Wrongs staff in front of Honey Bee's restaurant. Lehigh Valley, Pa., Sept. 5, 2021. From left: Ebube Nwaeme, Serafina Kennedy, Jesse Marsh, Cat Oriel, Doris Turkel (Writing Wrongs/Alliana Myers)

1941

During World War II, the Tuskegee Airmen were the first Black servicemen allowed to become pilots in the U.S. military. Under President Franklin D. Roosevelt, a segregated unit was created. Pilots were trained at the Tuskegee Army Air Field in Alabama to fly single-engine planes. The program was later expanded to include flight and crew training on two-engine B-25 bombers. A total of 992 pilots graduated from the Tuskegee Air Field program. They flew 1,578 missions and won more than 850 medals.[48]

THE GREAT COMMISSION

By Tiersa Curry

After the Sunday service cleared out, I made my way up the stairs to the second floor and began to hear children's laughter and footsteps. As I got to the top, I was greeted by a pair of preschoolers, and not far behind was Donnell Bowie. A tall Black man with a serious face, he could not hide his affection towards the children even while admonishing them over their horseplay through the pews. Most Christian people attend church on Sundays as it is seen as the principal day of communal worship; but more often than not, Bowie can be found at St. John African Methodist Episcopal (AME) Zion Church seven days out of the week. Raised in Asheville, North Carolina, 73-year-old Donnell Bowie has been a parishioner of St. John AME for roughly 25 years; he moved to the Lehigh Valley in 1973 and never left.

Bowie arrived at Lehigh University planning to study history but wound up in the program for secondary education; he became a middle-school social studies teacher, working for 31 years in the Allentown School District (ASD), as well as a student teacher supervisor at Kutztown University of Pennsylvania for half of a semester after his retirement. He recalled that closer to the beginning of his career in the ASD, the curriculum featured some cultural competency requirements allowing teachers to honor and teach Black History Month while also celebrating the multitude of cultures present by holding activities where the students could bring in and share a dish connected to their respective cultures. As state regulations shifted, teachers began to prioritize standardized tests over cultural pride and acceptance. He said, "The state regulations changed a lot. So [the teachers] may not have had the opportunity to [have] academic freedom."

Bowie's mentorship had an impact on his students. He took them out into the world and facilitated creative life experiences in the form of Pennsylvania History Day. For this event, Bowie's students visited Pennsylvania State University, Millersville University of Pennsylvania, or other colleges or universities in the state to learn about history and do historical research.

During his time working in the ASD, Bowie felt that his experiences as one of the few Black teachers in a predominately white school were "for the most part, good," and he expressed that he felt a sense of camaraderie among many of his fellow teachers no matter their race or ethnicity. But even though he felt accepted, Bowie found that in many instances he was being tasked with "speaking for or defending [himself] and the Black community." Black students were the third-largest racial group in the area when Bowie taught in the ASD; approximately more than 80% of the area identified as white, around 15% identified as Hispanic or Latino of any race, and less than 5% identified as Black.

Although his overarching experiences in the ASD were satisfactory, there were a few unfavorable incidents that took place during his time as a teacher. Being singled out and put on the spot numerous times by one white parent is a prominent memory in Bowie's mind. In one incident, a mother confronted him about the curriculum he was teaching in one of his classes. She questioned his teaching abilities and attempted to demean Bowie by telling him how to do his job, without understanding the curriculum herself. Another such incident occurred before the teachers and students left for Thanksgiving break. Bowie was called into a meeting with the same parent, as well as another student's mother, where they berated and bombarded him with questions regarding his work ethic and capabilities as a chaperone on a school trip to Washington, D.C. Although he was not the only chaperone, the mothers singled out and accused Bowie of neglecting their children and letting them run off without adult supervision. There is a carefully wrought history behind the ways white women weaponize their race and femininity while playing a central role as accusers and consequently instigators in the deaths of Black American

1942

In World War II, over 400 Native American men from 19 different tribes are recruited to the U.S. Marine Corps to develop and employ coded messages to the Allies via radio and telephone. These code talkers play a crucial role in capturing Iwo Jima. The military continues to use the code talkers after the war; their work remains classified and the public is largely unaware of their service even after declassification in 1968. Congressional Gold Medals are awarded to the Navajo code talkers in 2001. The Code Talker Recognition Act in 2002 honors the Sioux, Comanche, and Choctaw code talkers. Additional gold medals are awarded to other code talkers in 2008 and 2013.[49]

men. These types of incidents are not frozen in the past but have continued to occur to Bowie throughout his lifetime.

During our interview, Bowie gave an example of a recent microaggression where the validity of his credit was tested. He and his wife visited a local jewelry store to pick up their order, which came to a total of $105. When Bowie presented payment with a check, the woman behind the counter asked her employer if she should accept it. Assuming that Bowie was trying to give them a check that would bounce shows the subtle racism that seeps into the American consciousness. For many Black Americans, this situation can become a fraught experience that can lead to suspicious employees summoning the police. He mentions that the owner looked at him, as if to size him up or assume his socioeconomic status, but Bowie didn't care; he knew that check wasn't going to bounce. This degrading and dehumanizing encounter focuses on the relationship between respect and race. Racial profiling completely erases the humanity of Black Americans in that living their normal lives becomes a cause for suspicion. The shop owner's immediate hesitancy in providing Bowie with the goods he paid for displays both the shop owner's ignorance of the fact that Bowie's "money is still green" and his focus on the fact that Bowie's skin is not white.

When asked if racism presents itself more subtly or overtly with respect to our current political climate, Bowie said that racism is "too open." Although the number of anti-racist social movements and organizations have skyrocketed, the number of racist hate groups has flourished as well. The phrase "Make America Great Again" is not new and has been used by numerous politicians in their campaigns. This use of American nationalism is meant to recall all the different ways the United States of America has stood tall as the "land of the free and the home of the brave." Bowie and others in historically marginalized communities see the phrase for what it is — a decree for the United States to not become "great again, but white again."

Referencing the Capitol insurrection, Bowie declared that the incident "was an attack on democracy" and cited the lack of intervention by politicians, stating that they "[don't] want to do anything, because [they want] to remain in power." Although those who participated in the event have been identified and charged, many people feel that if Black people stormed the Capitol, not many would have made it out alive. These stark differences can be seen throughout the United States regarding policing and police violence and its relationship with Black lives. Movements such as #BlackLivesMatter and #SayHerName have highlighted Black consciousness and experiences, and Bowie stated that through this, Black people "became a voice in the political

> As one of the few Black teachers in a predominately white school, I was speaking for myself or defending myself ... and the Black community.

world that [white politicians] can't handle." Just as with the Capitol insurrection, politicians have continued to overlook areas of concern in the United States, such as the COVID-19 pandemic, which disproportionately affects marginalized communities of color.

The lack of government intervention also worked as a contributing factor in the polarization and politicization of the COVID-19 virus and vaccines. When asked about the importance of the vaccinations in Black communities, Bowie immediately expressed that "because most Black people who live in urban areas are in close contact or quarters," the vaccination is a necessity. He cited the mistrust the Black community feels towards the medical community, especially with the history of racist experiments where Black people were the subjects, such as the Tuskegee Experiment, but contends that this situation is different. Black Americans account for greater than 15% of COVID death victims but only make up around 12% of the American population, and Bowie expressed that "[the virus] affects the Black community wholly and heavily." Because of its widespread availability, he feels there is no excuse to not be vaccinated. He specifically references the work many Black churches have been doing all over the country volunteering to hand out vaccinations and remarked that Black Americans need to take advantage of that.

Bowie speaks highly of Black churches, especially regarding their contributions to the community during the pandemic, and Bowie's life history can be linked to the long history of St. John AME and its place in the Black

1943

The Zoot Suit, a fashion style consisting of high-waisted pants and a long coat with wide lapels, is worn by many Mexican-American youth. In addition to being prejudicially associated with gang violence and criminality, zoot suits are considered unpatriotic, against masculinity norms, and a challenge to "Juan Crow" laws. In what becomes known as the Zoot Suit Riots, groups of soldiers and sailors stationed in Los Angeles, along with civilians, routinely attack and beat zoot-suit-wearing youth for five days.[50]

community of Bethlehem. The old cobblestone building sits on a one-way street with parking on both sides. St. John has served its community for over 100 years as Lehigh Valley's first all-Black church. AME churches came about because of the necessity for a Western religious denomination that did not discriminate based on race. This site served as a birthplace for Black excellence in the community; Bethlehem's first Black teachers, its first Black principal, nurses, business owners, store clerks, and others all have ties to St. John AME Zion church. Founded in 1894 by Black families looking to create a space for themselves, their mission is "to move the people of God to higher heights by offering training, teaching, and preaching of God's word that addresses the spiritual, social, economic, and educational needs of the community." Demographically, the surrounding area was predominately white; but today, South Bethlehem is predominately Hispanic.

Currently, St. John AME has around 40 members in its congregation, with the median age being around 50 to 60-years old. Members live throughout the Lehigh Valley, in Bethlehem, Allentown, and Easton, even spanning into eastern New Jersey. The members of St. John AME make up an intimate group and are very active in the surrounding community. They work with the Bethlehem Emergency Shelter outsourced by the Cathedral Church of the Nativity by providing food, clothing, and toiletries; this past summer, they donated 22 cases of water, an item the shelter often runs out of. They have also participated in city-run events, singing at one of the Christmas tree lightings. Before the COVID-19 pandemic, members of St. John AME would donate materials and offer back-to-school supplies, not just for the student church members, but also to any kids who wanted or needed them, with over 100 students receiving supplies each year. Bowie praises the positive and gratifying work the church has done. St. John AME has been an incredibly important institution, not only in the church community but in the Black history of Bethlehem as a whole.

Within the church, Black excellence is revered. Bowie mentioned that for Black History Month, the kids created a presentation showcasing Black people's achievements entitled "'A Moment in Black History' at the pulpit. It ran from February to maybe the end of March, because there [were] a lot of kids doing it, many of the youth in the congregation." Yet, membership is down for a number of reasons including the COVID-19 pandemic as well as lack of parishioners between the ages of 20 and 30. Bowie laments that those who came up in the church are now grown and out in the world, but hopes to not only "improve [his] own relationship with God" but to also "try to bring other people along with [him], which is the Great Commission." Although he enjoys how close-knit the congregation is, Bowie's goal for the church is to "go and have a bigger edifice than ever."

The alter at St. John AME Zion Church. Bethlehem, Pa., Sept 5, 2021. (Writing Wrongs/Alliana Myers)

1945

Under the order of President Harry S. Truman, the United States drops two nuclear bombs on the Japanese cities of Hiroshima and Nagasaki, instantly killing as many as 110,000 people, most of whom are civilians. In the years that follow, hundreds of thousands more suffer and die from devastating radiation-related illnesses.[51]

40 WRITING WRONGS

Dominick Boyd, Owner of Born Into The Arts dance studio, Allentown, Pa., takes part in a speaker panel at the sixth Writing Wrongs program. Bethlehem, Pa., Sept. 5, 2021. (Writing Wrongs/Jennifer Berrios)

1950

To stymie the spread of communism, the U.S. intervenes in the conflict between North and South Korea, the first overseas deployment with a desegregated American military. About 600,000 Black Americans, nicknamed the Buffalo Soldiers, serve in the Korean War. Nine percent of Americans killed there are Black.[52]

BRINGING THE BOOGIE-DOWN BRONX TO THE LEHIGH VALLEY

By Doris Turkel

Dominick Boyd was born into hip-hop, literally. Boyd grew up in the Bronx, New York City — 1520 Sedgwick Avenue, to be exact. This building has been coined the "birthplace of hip-hop" because of the original rhyming and record spinning hip-hop sound that DJ Kool Herc introduced at parties in its common room. Boyd found his joy for dancing outside of his apartment building, listening to artists like Michael Jackson with his sister and friends.

Full of life and as passionate about hip-hop dance as ever, Boyd has now owned his Allentown, Pennsylvania dance studio, Born Into The Arts, for thirteen years. His teaching philosophy: Dance is "a small part of the lesson."

As a teenager, Boyd was scouted to join the dance agency, Teens in Motion, through which he was able to work with musical artists like Alicia Keys, compete in dance competitions with other youth, and even perform at the Grammys. However, Boyd found his true role in the dance world when he landed a job with the New York City Housing Authority and began teaching hip-hop dance to children and youth in housing projects and community centers across Brooklyn and Queens. In these rec rooms is where Boyd found his passion for teaching. He felt how much respect his students had for him and realized that his dance classes could impact youth in vast ways. "Once I found that, I fell in love. My students were so important to me," Boyd said.

Boyd eventually made the move to Pennsylvania to escape the hustle and bustle of the city and because he thought that it was hard to succeed in such a competitive and pressured environment. Boyd began teaching in different studios throughout the Lehigh Valley — what he described as his first culture shock — mostly because Bronx hip-hop was foreign to rural Pennsylvania. Boyd explained that local dance competitions lacked a hip-hop category, offering "jamming" instead. Boyd laughs, "They had people doing toe touches — I was just so confused!"

However, Boyd doesn't credit his dance studio with bringing hip-hop to the area. He noticed hip-hop dance engrained in other types of dancing at local clubs and studios, including breakdancing, ballet, and tap dance. At first, Boyd felt like he didn't have the freedom to teach the way he wanted, using the music he liked. When he opened his own dance studio, he was the "only person [in Lehigh County] who taught real hip-hop choreography."

Moving to rural Pennsylvania from New York City was at times disorienting for Boyd, as he felt like an emphasis was placed on his race, explaining: "I never dealt with racism — I grew up in New York; it's not like that. It's separated

> **Boyd believed that hip-hop could be a uniting force in the Lehigh Valley as a genre reflective of Black history, innovation, and resilience.**

1954

The Supreme Court decision in Brown v. The Board of Education renders racial segregation in schools unconstitutional, overturning the "separate but equal" precedent set by Plessy v. Ferguson.[53]

Dominick Boyd (left) and Matthew Riddick speak to the Writing Wrongs group. Bethlehem, Pa., Sept. 5, 2021. (Writing Wrongs/Jennifer Berrios)

in a way, in New York, but it's not segregated like it is here. I notice certain comments that remind me that I'm not just a teacher — I'm a Black guy."

Although New York City is racially diverse, Boyd feels that there is more interracial socializing in Allentown, partly as a result of the residential stratification in NYC. However, minorities in Allentown are also limited in their opportunities because of generational socioeconomic constraints. "It's a natural thing; everybody stays in their pocket. I think the segregation in certain areas is because the majority of ethnic people here are put under stereotypes, so they stay at a lower bracket. A lot of [minority] people here are struggling financially," Boyd said.

Boyd believed that hip-hop could be a uniting force in the Lehigh Valley as a genre reflective of Black history, innovation, and resilience. Boyd explained, "The beautiful part about what hip-hop is is based on true African American history, and who we are from the jump. Everything about us was creation; we created off of nothing. Hip-hop represents taking nothing and making it into something. From slavery, stuffing chicken with collard greens — that was the bad stuff that when they cooked they threw out and gave to the slaves. We put the flavor in and we took what we had. From slavery, when slaves were whipped, they used to sing. We took the worst position, and the same energy we put in hip-hop. When the Bronx was known as the burnt-down Bronx, we took disco, and we had that one person that liked the sound of the record when it stopped — that created the scratch. Then someone connected the bridge of two songs and made it a repeated beat and a new rhythm. We created these things off of what we had around us."

As the first Black-owned hip-hop dance studio in the area, Born Into The Arts is a diverse community, teaching students from age 4 to adults, with a variety of backgrounds and races. "These are the things about the culture that I'm trying to bring to this area. This is how you could use people's minds. This is how you could learn who we are, understand these children. ... This is how we could unify with each other," Boyd explained. Most important to Boyd is that his studio is a place where students feel comfortable. However, Boyd's studio still faces microaggressions at competitions, where his team is stereotyped because of their diversity. Boyd said, "My kids are no joke, but we still couldn't get away from 'Oh, that's that ghetto studio.' My kids were good kids."

Still, Boyd works seven days a week to share the joy of dance with the Lehigh Valley community and thinks that we could all benefit from a dance class.

"When a good song comes, you're not looking at the person next to you thinking, 'You're white, I'm Black, you're this, you're that.' You're just expressing," Boyd said. "Use your struggles, use your surroundings, and create an art form out of it."

1955 Emmett Till (1941–1955), a Black 14-year-old, is murdered in Mississippi after being falsely accused of whistling at a white woman. An all-white jury acquits the two men accused of the crime. The images of Till's beaten and maimed body shocks many Americans, spurring them to protest racial injustice.[54]

GRIT AND RESILIENCE:
An Evolution of the Black Church in the Lehigh Valley

St. John AME Zion Church entrance. Bethlehem, Pa., Sept, 5, 2021. (Writing Wrongs/Jennifer Berrios)

By Kylie Stoltzfus

A humble stone church located in the heart of the city of Bethlehem, Pennsylvania houses nearly 150 years of Black history. Founded in 1894, St. John African Methodist Episcopal (AME) Zion Church is the oldest African American church in the city. It was also the first African American church in the Lehigh Valley. St. John has seen members of its congregation contribute to the Bethlehem community, leaving a profound impact on the city. According to its website, the church has produced generations of leaders who have broken barriers in the United States: "Our church has sprung many community leaders, such as Bethlehem's first Black teachers, the first Black principal, nurses, business owners, store clerks, and others."

Winston Alozie is a historian at St. John AME Zion Church. Alozie uses his love of history to preserve the rich legacy that presides in Bethlehem, hoping to pass it on to future generations

As Alozie continued to learn about people who were part of Black progress in Bethlehem, he was inspired by their stories. Alozie began asking questions to gain a greater picture of the story that was embedded in the town where he lived.

"As a Black person that moved to this area. I thought that there was very little history here. So to find out that there is — just people weren't talking about it, or wasn't written down, or, you know, nobody knew it — to me, that was mind blowing," Alozie said. "I wanted to be able to share and give that information to whoever needs to have it for whatever purposes. And hopefully, I'm not the only person that will do that. But specifically for this congregation here, I hold that position with a high honor. I want to do it with the best integrity and fidelity that I can."

The congregation is predominantly older folks aged 60 and above. Alozie, 33, views himself as a curator of the congregation's history: "In being the historian here, one of the things that I found amazing is that the timeline of this congregation is congruent with the timeline of Black progress in the United States."

1957

Racial integration in American schools begins, starting with the Little Rock Nine at Central High in Little Rock, Arkansas.[55] Three years later, Ruby Bridges (1954–) follows at William Frantz Elementary School in New Orleans, Louisiana.[56]

Winston Alozie, CEO of the Boys and Girls Club of Bethlehem, serves as the historian of St. John AME Zion Church. Bethlehem, Pa., Sept. 5, 2021. (Writing Wrongs/Alliana Myers)

The Civil Rights Movement in the United States led to a civil rights coalition in Bethlehem led by members of the St. John congregation. St. John has always been a small church in both its physical structure and its congregation. Its period of largest membership was during the 1950s and '60s in the middle of the Civil Rights Movement.

"People were drawn to what was happening here," Alozie said. "You get to see Black history from a national context, but then you get to see the same from a local context here in Lehigh Valley."

Alozie said that prior to St. John, there were other instances where people tried to organize congregations. Social groups would form in hopes of starting a church, but they fizzled out before long. St. John was an attempt at building community which gained traction, came together, and put their vision into practice.

"When you have a sense of community, you have a sense of space where you are affirmed, you are seen, you are heard, you are valued," Alozie said. "To have a place where that can happen, especially for people who belong to various

1961

Four hundred volunteers travel on regularly scheduled interstate buses throughout the South as "Freedom Riders" to test a 1960 Supreme Court decision that declared segregated travel illegal. Many travelers are assaulted and/or arrested.[57]

marginalized groups, to be in a space that champions you for being you gives you all, in my opinion, the empowerment that you need. You have wind in your sails; you've got people that believe in you and say that you can do it."

St. John expresses its mission as "[hoping] to move people of God to higher heights by offering training, teaching, and preaching of God's word that addresses spiritual, social, economic, and educational needs of the community."

Talking about the perception of the Black Church, Alozie said that a surface level view can create stereotypes that sell short the gravity of what this community represents. When many people think of the Black church, they may think of happy Black people singing or Black grandmothers praying for prodigal grandchildren. He sees these generalizations as shallow portrayals of what the church embodies.

Alozie describes his role as a member of the congregation and historian at St. John as investing in the present day to create a legacy that lasts for future generations.

"Whatever you're involved in existed before you got there and will be there after. And if you are the creator of something, you should be building something that's sustainable after you," Alozie said. "That's why I'm part of this congregation. It existed for 110 years before I got here and I'm hopeful and I believe that it will be in existence 110 years after I'm gone."

The resilience of the St. John community is evident when Alozie reviews the church's historical documents and sees the list of names and signatures from people who have held a place in the congregation, and when exploring United States census data or cemetery records. He compares the struggles of the Black Church to that of the Jewish people, believing that one of the beautiful things about the Black Church is how its struggle has shaped its ability to see humanity in a new light.

"God is the God of those people who have been marginalized," Alozie said. "God is a God [of] other people who've been hurt and harmed. And when we see that, we then reciprocate that love that God shows us to others."

A newspaper clipping in the St. John archive highlights actor and activist Paul Robeson's visit to Bethlehem. Robeson was famous for both his cultural accomplishments and his political stances. Bethlehem, Pa., Sept. 5, 2021. (Writing Wrongs/Alliana Myers)

When he watched elderly women with physical impairments crawl up the stairs from the front of the church to the sanctuary just to be with their community, Alozie was awestruck by the grit and tenacity of his congregation.

"I want that same fervor and [fire] when I'm 80," Alozie said. "To crawl into where I belong and where I [am] supposed to be because I see value in it."

"The Black story is long; it is different. It is colorful; it is complicated. But it is a story [that] no matter at what point you touch that timeline, no matter what slice of the cake you take, it is rich with progress. It is rich with determination. And it is rich with resilience," Alozie said. "I pray every day that God gives me that resilience."

1963 Dr. Rev. Martin Luther King Jr. (1929–1968) writes his influential "Letter from Birmingham Jail" after being imprisoned for a nonviolent protest against segregation.[58] This same year, he delivers his famous "I Have A Dream" speech at the March on Washington for Jobs and Freedom.[59]

INNOCENCE AND REVELATION:

The Moravian Community of Bethlehem

The Moravian Cemetery (1742-1910) in downtown Bethlehem, also known as "God's Acre," is one of the oldest perpetually maintained cemeteries in the U.S. Because of the Moravians' belief that everyone is equal in death, only flat headstones were allowed. Bethlehem, Pa., Sept. 5, 2021. (Writing Wrongs/Shannon O'Connor)

1964 — Malcolm X (1925–1965), Black Nationalist civil rights leader, gives his infamous "The Ballot or the Bullet" speech, encouraging Black Americans to vote. He is assassinated in Omaha, Nebraska at the age of 39.[60]

By Natalie Dang and Luka Marjanovic

This is the Moravian Church. Not Monrovian. Moravian. All along Bethlehem's Main Street, plaques adorn the sidewalks and buildings, reminding pedestrians of the influence that Moravians had on the German-inspired edifices. What is hidden from plain view is that the Moravians actually founded the city in 1741. Also, it's pronounced Mo-RAY-vee-an. However, beneath the lustrous foundations hides a haunting circumstance upon which the city was built.

Pastor Christine Johnson has lived in Bethlehem on and off throughout her life. She moved back to Bethlehem about two years ago with her husband, both working as pastors at churches within the community. Although her latest stint has been just two years now, Johnson first came to Bethlehem 35 years ago to study at the Moravian Theological Seminary. The path that led her to the seminary began when she was a child. Her family attended church regularly, cultivating in her a deep bond with God — a bond that would follow the Pastor throughout her life.

When Johnson was 15, her family uprooted her from their hometown in Wisconsin. Devastated that she had to move away from the comfort and familiarity of the town she knew so well, Johnson asked God what she was supposed to do. The answer: God wanted her to become a minister. Although she had interests in writing, theater, and music, eventually graduating from college with a major in English and a minor in music, she could never shake off the calling she had received so many years previously. In time, Johnson came to the Moravian Theological Seminary where she obtained her Master of Divinity degree in 1988. From there she preached for multiple congregations and is now a pastor at College Hill Moravian Church. In this work, Johnson is able to combine the interests she cultivated in her undergraduate studies with her divine calling.

The morning of our interview, she had just held a Sunday service sharing the teachings and values of the Moravian Church. When asked about the core values of their teachings, Johnson recited the phrase, "God creates. God redeems. God sustains." She mentioned that "God can do what God does in the world but if people don't respond, it doesn't really necessarily go anywhere and if [people] respond negatively, it doesn't necessarily spread good news in any way." Another phrase that Johnson dubs her "catchphrase" is this: "In essentials unity, in nonessentials liberty, but in all things love." She emphasized that love is the force that compels people to act on the teachings of the Church. These actions give hope that everyone can be seen as equals in God's eyes.

1964

The Civil Rights Act of 1964 prohibits federal and state discrimination on the basis of race, color, creed, class, and religion. This strengthens desegregation.[61]

The Rev. Christine Johnson. Bethlehem, Pa., Sept. 5, 2021. (Writing Wrongs/Shannon O'Connor)

The sentiment of equality rang clear in Johnson's words as she spoke about the values of the Moravian Church. "There's nothing that should divide us," she said. "There's a lot of stuff you can let go of because it might be your taste but not necessarily your core." Her distinction between "tastes" and "core" brings insight to how we might be able to approach our world today. It is true that we all have different "tastes," but difference of opinions should not become an impenetrable force that divides us all. If we can find a way to let go of these differences and search for what is essential to our core, then perhaps we can move forward towards a more equal society.

This way of thinking can be seen in the founding of Bethlehem, Pennsylvania, in 1741. Now a city of over 75,000 people, Bethlehem was founded when a small congregation of European immigrants settled on the land of what is Bethlehem today. They brought with them the teachings and practices of the Moravian Church. According to Johnson, who was very open to discussing the history of Moravians in America, the Moravian Church expanded to Western Pennsylvania and Ohio, launching mission efforts to offer their message to Native Americans. She proceeded in a more conversational manner, stating that the Moravian ideals were to share their teachings only to those who were interested in the religion, rather than forcing others to comply. This would mark only the beginning of a long, and many would say positive, Moravian history on the grounds of Bethlehem.

Johnson continued with the fact that "Moravians set up shop on what is Main Street now," which today is filled with candy stores, wineries, and a hotel, a modern parallel to the craft and trade shops that were a part of 1700s Bethlehem. If one were to walk further down the same street, they would reach what was once the industrial end of town; and its purpose never changed, only became more modernized.

Along those lines, Johnson described what that street looked like three hundred years ago, when it functioned more communally and cooperatively: "On the industrial end of town there were blacksmiths and potters." People farmed, and depending on their necessity, one could also hold a job here. "It was a really successful community and in that sense, everybody had something to do because it supported the work of the missionaries who would go out to Ohio, or just out into the middle of nowhere, to share the Gospel," Johnson continued. "Somebody in Bethlehem was always working to financially support them. People would sell outside the community to support fundraising for the work of the church." The process of giving all of one's earnings back to the community was known as the General Economy. This was also known as the most prosperous period of the Moravian community in the Pennsylvanian Bethlehem. The core values of cooperativeness and communitarianism remain within the teachings and operations of the Moravian church today, but not to this extent.

This prosperous period most definitely ended during the American Revolution. Johnson noted, "When George Washington and all his folks were swarming around Bethlehem, Moravians built a bar and a hotel on the other end of town to keep the troops out of the main area of the city." The Moravians continued offering aid to outsiders and their own community, but the communal groups that once

1965

Martin Luther King Jr. (1929–1968) leads three nonviolent protest marches from Selma to Montgomery, Alabama in response to the murder of activist Jimmie Lee Johnson and policies that hinder the Black right to vote. When the unarmed group of about 600 attempts to cross the Edmund Pettus Bridge during the first march (Bloody Sunday), they are brutally beaten and sprayed with tear gas by state and local police. King is assassinated in Memphis, Tennessee at the age of 39.

existed and the General Economy that pushed its society forward never returned to its former glory. When the Central Moravian Church was completed in 1806, it was, according to Johnson, the "biggest freestanding structure in the country at the time," adding that it was "the period of time in the country when things [were] getting bigger, and bigger things [were] being built." Johnson suspects that this expansion is one of the reasons why the communal way of living never returned and why Bethlehem started turning away from its founding ideals towards a more traditional American settlement. The community grew, outsiders came in, new churches and religions joined, and this meant that traditions were being left behind as progress took over and the world moved forward. The togetherness that made the Moravian society so attractive in the beginning disappeared somewhere along the historical path.

The Pastor did not shy away from showcasing some of the potential flaws within the original Moravian community as well. "As much as we practice hospitality, I think initially it was like, 'We'll be nice to you, we'll be your trading partners, but we don't know if you want to be in the village,'" she said. Johnson kept giving voice to the ancient Moravians to illustrate how she is modernizing classical Moravian values.

But, the Moravians did not completely isolate themselves: "In the Revolutionary War, the Moravians wouldn't take sides; they wouldn't side with the British or with the Americans, but they provided respite; they provided hospital care because of the battles raging in the area." After the Revolutionary War, as the world grew larger, the Moravians had to expand as well. Johnson explained this as the natural course of evolution that the Moravian society in Bethlehem had to face. They had to change with the world or be left behind.

The communal way of living "didn't really turn out to be sustainable for a terribly long amount of time. Eventually people get married, start families; they don't go into the mission field, and then the community does change," said Johnson. She continued to explain that the Moravian missionaries would get married so that they would not be wandering out into the fields alone, "but eventually you got more couples than you've got jobs, and it naturally evolved into people moving away and never returning to the communal way of living." The modern world had forced assimilation upon everybody and everything, and that did not exclude the Moravians of Bethlehem, Pennsylvania.

"The Moravian General Economy certainly didn't survive into the modern world and in whole, but I think those concepts have stuck with us for a long time, as well as the notion of wanting to take care of one another,"

explained Johnson. The Moravian church still does fundraising for the churches that were destroyed in Haiti, for the Afghanistan refugees, and for any people in need within its own local community.

When talking about how the community of Bethlehem today compares to when Bethlehem was first founded, Johnson noted that it "all depends on what people want to get out of it, and what they are willing to put into it." She gave examples of a Moravian Community in North Philadelphia that fixes up rundown houses and opens up t-shirt shops in order to give employment to people in less developed areas in Philly. They rebuild block by block, just like the Moravians expanded block by block in the 1700s and onward.

Johnson also talked about the church's adaptation to COVID-19 restrictions, and how they set up transmitters that would allow churchgoers to follow a service outside of the church in the safety of their cars, beeping to acknowledge their presence and faith. She mentioned neighborhoods in Madison, Wisconsin, where multiple families would share one car, or groups of seniors without family or children roomed together like college students and took care of each other. The world is seemingly full of small-scale 1700s Bethlehems, and one just has to look hard enough to find a small corner of communal living and aid. Johnson did note that "Free enterprise is also a hallmark of this nation; making a buck is just as part of our founding as being noble, so those are side-by-side values. On the church side we just try to make sure the values we aspire to, we also follow once in a while. And if we can lead by example, cool." Johnson is not blind to the realities of the world we are all living in, but she remains optimistic in the good nature of people as well as that we can only improve and become better.

She pointed out that the original Moravians in Bethlehem had universal healthcare and equal educational rights for both men and women. She cited progressive John Amos Comenius, a European and Moravian philosopher, as somebody who was a huge proponent of educational equality when it comes to gender and who fought for a more varied education. He is also the reason why we have recess in our schools, which she pointed out with glee and pride. She talked about the Moravian Book Shop in Bethlehem, founded in 1745, the oldest bookstore in the United States, as another source of education originated by Moravians in this world, which she presumes was founded for the same reasons that the aforementioned blacksmiths and potters had such a big impact on the 1700s Moravian society — its educational craft and making money.

1965 In a controversial attempt to prevent the spread of communism, the U.S. enters the Vietnam War. Approximately 300,000 African Americans serve in Vietnam, comprising 31% of ground combat troops. More than 80,000 Hispanic Americans also serve, along with 42,000 Native Americans and 35,000 Asian Americans. The war continues until 1975.[63]

Despite all these positive impacts the Moravian community had on this specific area of the United States, it shares some negative aspects of U.S. history as well. Johnson ended the interview with an admission that is as brutally honest as it is encouraging: "I feel like I'm dishonest if I don't share this with you. These are all our ideals, and we do not always succeed in following them. Some of our historians and local seminary professors have been doing research and have discovered that Moravians did have slaves, especially in North Carolina where they raised tobacco on plantations; and some people in Bethlehem had slaves as well. I want to tell myself we treated them better than everyone else was treated, but I don't know if that's true. I don't know that it was really widespread, but it's certainly not a part of the story anybody started telling until about two years ago. And so now we're trying to learn what to do with that, so I don't want to pass us off as if we've always been perfect, and we do have ideals, but we haven't always lived up to them. So, sure — in death, we're all equal, but in life, maybe not so much. But we try, many of us." She ended by saying that the whole clergy is working on finding ways to acknowledge their past mistakes, even if that means apologizing. They are all learning and working to uphold these ideals better in their present and future.

According to an article by Jon F. Sensbach called "Race and the Early Moravian Church: A Comparative Perspective" published by the Moravian Historical Society, "These men and women, enslaved though they were, entered the Moravian congregational family and were addressed as 'Brother' and 'Sister' like any white worshiper. Just as thoroughly as any European, they absorbed themselves into the church's intricate web of social relations, particularly the choir system. African men and women lived in the Single Brothers' and Single Sisters' houses in Bethlehem and Salem, where they worked, worshiped, ate, and slept dormitory-style together with white brothers and sisters. Black congregants took Communion, attended choir meetings and festivals, sat on church benches, and exchanged the kiss of peace with whites. Occasionally in the workplace they held managerial positions, even supervising white Brethren." Still, no matter how their position is painted in academic writing, this does not change the fact that they were slaves, and no amount of rationalizing can make slavery acceptable. What we can glean from this unsightly part of Moravian history is that no retelling of the past should be taken as a fact. This discovery made by present Moravian Church leaders should serve as a lesson and further showcase that

The Rev. Christine Johnson (center) speaks with Staff Writers Luka Marjanovic (left) and Natalie Dang about the history of the Moravian Church in Bethlehem, Pennsylvania. Bethlehem, Pa., Sept. 5, 2021. (Writing Wrongs/Shannon O'Connor)

1965

The Immigration and Naturalization Act of 1965 removes the old quota system, which had limited the amount of immigrants who could enter the U.S. from outside Western Europe. Immigration officials focus on reuniting immigrant families and encouraging labor migration. This Act creates immigration opportunities for highly skilled Asians and/or those with family already in the U.S.[64]

> The Moravian General Economy certainly didn't survive into the modern world and in whole, but I think those concepts have stuck with us for a long time, as well as the notion of wanting to take care of one another.

everything should be questioned; nothing should be taken for granted without thorough research.

Johnson stands behind her belief that the neutrality of the Moravian Church represented the best aspect of their history, saying that "We sought to be peaceful." Perhaps to some, neutrality in the modern day regarding issues such as racism could be seen as turning a blind eye. But not taking sides does not necessarily mean that we will resort to becoming a color-blind society. The Moravian Church's effort to acknowledge past wrongs shows accountability in past actions. However, a sense of neutrality could also prove to be beneficial in an ever-polarizing society. Often, when we take a side, we forget to listen to what others are saying. Cultivating the patience to listen to opinions outside of our own and taking the time to truly understand where these opinions come from can open the door to transformational conversations.

In a large grassy area, nestled between the quaint buildings of Bethlehem, is the Moravian Cemetery. At first glance, one would not assume that this is a cemetery. But as you walk through what looks like a park, you will notice plaques lined side by side along the grassy floor — each plaque the same size and shape as the one next to it. Johnson explains that in the Moravian tradition, all people are buried equally under identical flat tombstones, emphasizing "the idea of not building monuments to any person, because in God's eyes, we are all equal." As we walked through the cemetery, we saw the names of people of white, Black, and Native American descent intermingled throughout, seeming to echo Johnson's words: "In death, we are equal, but in life, maybe not so much. But we try, many of us." The time has come where we should no longer wait until death to be equal. As we continue our efforts in creating a just and equal society — where those living side by side are not divided by the color of their skin — we can remember the visual truth seen in this cemetery as a hallmark of a history that is worth learning from.

The Christmas City Mansion, West Church St., served as the headquarters for the sixth Writing Wrongs program. Bethlehem, Pa., Sept. 5, 2021. (Writing Wrongs/Gayle F. Hendricks)

1971

President Richard Nixon (1913–1994) declares a "War on Drugs," expanding the Drug Abuse Prevention and Control Act (1970), which initiated the use of no-knock warrants by police. Nixon's policy is based on racially biased ideas about certain drugs and drug users, leading to the disproportionate criminalization of Black and Brown Americans.[65]

A MAN WITH A HEART FOR STORIES

By Chekwube Okunowo

Darin Barron, a native of New Jersey, tells the tale of his development and the ideals that shaped him into becoming the filmmaker, producer, and dancer he is today. He told the story of his love for people regardless of their backgrounds and spoke on how passionate he is about spreading inspiration in any way he can. To begin, he spoke of his early days in Newark, growing up in a Jehovah's Witness home where he was indoctrinated into the culture of going door-to-door, evangelizing.

That evangelizing process allowed him the opportunity of getting to know individuals in the community and understanding more about their life experiences. This level of understanding is, as Barron said, "how my love for people came into play." By having a strong grasp of the various things that different people go through regardless of the color of their skin or the culture they belong to or practice, Barron was able to understand at an early age that "being able to engage with people, to have love for people, to be around people, to help people, to support people, and to be able to show that love and not discriminate" was extremely important.

This is also connected to the reason why he holds very strong opinions against the use of the n-word slur by both Black people and non-Black people in everyday language or in the media. In his words, "It's a part of history, but it's a dark history." And it is his belief that including the derogatory remarks used against Black people during slavery does no one any good.

These aforementioned values served as the bedrock of Barron's career. In high school, he moved to the Bethlehem area where he wanted to get involved in the dance community. These values helped him network and make connections with people. However, Barron explains that even in making connections and adapting to the dance community, he faced challenges. People did not know him, and Barron had to assert his skill. He practiced more, signed up for dance teams, and even participated in competitions. This was how he was able to become a part of the community. By putting himself out there, he was able to show people what he was capable of. As a Black youth, the stakes were even higher because of the stereotype that Black people automatically have the ability to dance. For him, moving past that stereotype and focusing solely on his own craft as an individual was imperative to making a name for himself in the community, not just in regular dancing but also in the art of krumping.

Barron explained that in krumping, a street dance popular among African-Americans, being expressive and telling a story was the foundation of the art. Through the placement of the hands, eye contact, facial expressions and leg movements, a story is passed across to the audience. When asked about the predominant story he tells in his dance, he explained that he tries to "stay on ... the spiritual side" and incorporate the different things he has experienced. By telling these stories, he is also communicating with other

Darin Barron Jr., owner of Darin Barron Photography, participates in a panel of Lehigh Valley leaders who speak to the Writing Wrongs group. Bethlehem, Pa., Sept. 5, 2021. (Writing Wrongs/Alliana Myers)

1984

President Ronald Reagan (1911–2004) expands the "War onDrugs" in response to the crack cocaine epidemic. This devastates low-income urban communities and contributes to increased arrests, criminalization, poverty, and violence. By the late 1990s, approximately 85% of crack users are Black.[66] Mandatory minimum sentencing laws lead to racially disproportionate incarceration rates for nonviolent drug users, increasing from 50,000 in the early 1980s to 400,000 in 2005.[67]

individuals and this also helps, in its own way, to form connections with the audience.

With the various connections and relationships he made in the dance community, he was able to meet several filmmakers who served as doorways for him to get involved in filmmaking. He stated that the filmmakers walked him through the entirety of the process. They showed him how to edit; he expressed his excitement at the help they gave him. It was this enthusiasm for filmmaking that motivated Barron to create a film for the community called "Dance Wars," which was inspired by the artistry of Arthur Laurents' "West Side Story."

With multiple teams made up of playwrights, videographers and filmmakers, collegian Barron set up in a studio in Lehigh University for auditions and casting calls. "It was a really awesome experience because it really brought people together from all different walks of life," Barron said. Not only did it prove to be just an interesting experience for him, but it also informed Barron's decision to get involved in filmmaking.

Filmmaking led Barron to meet Hayden Craddolph, the executive director of Haydenfilms Institute, which is a nonprofit organization aimed at funding and educating independent filmmakers. By getting involved with this institution, Barron was able to connect with many individuals and community leaders. It also got him involved in projects like the Youth Media Initiative, which allowed him to "really get to know the community and the younger people."

Barron became involved with Haydenfilms' Youth Media Initiative, a program aimed at pulling young adults out of environments that did not encourage them to go for their dreams, which was in this case, Reading, Pennsylvania. The individuals were taken to Kutztown University where they were encouraged to bring their own personal stories to life through film, whether it focused on youth violence, drug abuse, poverty, or gang violence. And just like every other experience Barron had been through, he found it rewarding because of his ability to "engage with the community and really meet their parents, meet a lot of the different leaders in the community, and to really be a part of that."

As the years went by, Barron wanted to make use of the resources he had to create his own project. So, he created the "What's Your Story?" docuseries which would highlight "all people from different communities" regardless of their background — "business, education, music" or other walks of life.

He and his team would then carry out research on individuals making an impact in the society. They would also take referrals from other community members about the people they believed should be featured in the docuseries. After that, those whose works had been found worthy would have their organization, involvement, and impact in the community spotlighted. "Highlighting their business and highlighting their story really help us as a community to get to know each other," Barron said. When asked about the importance of get-ting to know the other members of the community, he stated simply, "Because these are some people that we patronize, we go to their stores, we go to their businesses. We don't really know them, but we do business with them."

Darin Barron Jr. demonstrates Krump, a style of African American street dance. Bethlehem, Pa., Sept. 5, 2021. (Writing Wrongs/Shannon O'Connor)

In a similar light, Barron also started the idea of the "My City" Dance Series which would only differ from the "What's Your Story?" docuseries in the sense that it would focus more on the dancers in the community. It would give them an opportunity to be filmed by a professional and have their skills showcased in a very official way typical of an expert dance portfolio.

It is also worthy of mention that for Barron, a key goal of the two docuseries would be to highlight the work of all the members of the community regardless of their differences. In his words, "It's also beautiful to see different races because you get different perspectives, you have different ideas, dif-ferent opinions." In other words, Barron is a man who is extremely passionate about diversity and the harmonious unity it brings societies. He emphasized that "it's important that we really focus on seeing the beauty in all people."

Today, Barron has made a name for himself in the Lehigh Valley as an individual committed to hearing and sharing the experiences of the extremely diverse members of the community. He has also asserted himself as an individual who is committed to putting in the work towards his craft, promoting positive and uplifting content in whatever way he can. He is constantly trying to motivate others, and that fuels his need to hear the stories of others and have his own story heard in turn. To Barron, inspiration can always be found in a story, and the impact that can have on those who pay attention is what he's excited about.

1985

Local government in Philadelphia bomb a row home in the city during a stand-off between police and a Black liberation group, MOVE. The incident kills six adults, five children, and destroys more than 60 homes.[68]

Staff Writer Sonjirose Chin interviews Kalief Robinson on Zoom. Bethlehem, Pa., Sept. 5, 2021. (Writing Wrongs/Shannon O'Connor)

1991

The beating of Rodney King (1965–2012) by Los Angeles Police Department officers is recorded by salesman George Holliday. The violence and the police officers' acquittal spark outrage, which leads to protests and riots in Los Angeles.[69]

US, THE DREAMERS

By Sonjirose Chin

Editor's Note: The author requested that readers listen to "Youth" by Glass Animals before reading this piece.

How many of us are dreamers? Even as we age out of days of lullabies, playing until the street lights glow, and dancing on our mothers' feet — how many of us hold on to that childlike fancy that anything and everything is possible, even as we grow into a world that often times does not understand us — the dreamers?

"My mom was always the realistic one; I was the dreamer," said Kalief Robinson, 31, a Brooklyn native. "Dance, to me, was my first love." Robinson's childhood was entangled with music and subsequently dance. A little boy with his heart thumping to the cadence of the melody, Robinson would waltz on the tops of his mother's feet, their souls melding into one as the oldies echoed throughout their twosome household — the birth of a lifelong passion for this little Black boy. Robinson recalled that he had to cope with responsibilities at an early age. He had his mother for emotional support, both sharing the kindred spirit of being "emotional people and wearing their hearts on their sleeves." She taught her child about vulnerability, which would translate into his dancing and strengthen him as he moved through the world as a Black man.

Robinson started out with street dancing, learning from television and studying his two idols, Michael Jackson and Usher. At age 12, Robinson moved to Bethlehem, Pennsylvania, and joined the Hispanic American League of Artists. There he found community in learning Latin dance, discovering Latin ballroom styles of salsa, merengue, bachata, samba, tango, and rhumba. Robinson started several dance groups in his high school.

Later, he joined Born Into the Arts, a dance studio in Allentown, mastering his craft until age 22 when he then taught dance classes at various studios. He was a master of soulful and suave footwork. Robinson created the first dance teams at Pennsylvania State University Lehigh Valley and participated in a 46-hour-long dance-a-thon for charity for pediatric cancer patients. In college, he studied business and marketing management; he credits his mother's influence for "bringing me back to reality," guiding Robinson to a possible backup plan if dancing did not work out.

Fortunately, dreams come true and passions flourish. In 2016, Robinson became the proud owner and operator of Precision Dance Studios, a family-owned studio in Whitehall, Pennsylvania. He named the studio "Precision" because of its dedication to time and patience with each individual, and working until the students "understood the art, understood the choreography, and were able to showcase." Robinson wants to provide an outlet for under-served communities of color; his classes are open to ages two and up, including parents and adults who are looking for a way to express themselves through dance.

He prides himself on making classes affordable and accessible, being one of the least expensive studios in the Lehigh Valley. Robinson declared, "We base our studio on the fact that we want to teach, not to make money." At times some people may see Precision as low quality because of its affordable price points and the classes focusing solely on "urban styles" because Robinson is a Black owner. He expresses that being a Black owner means his studio is not taken as seriously as white-owned studios, which dominate the dance sphere with more

1998

White Supremacist John William King and two other white men offer James Byrd Jr. (1949–1998), a Black man, a ride home in Jasper, Texas. They then spray-paint his face, beat him, chain him by his ankles to their truck, and drag him to his death. King was executed in 2019. In 2001, Texas passes the James Byrd Jr. Hate Crimes Act. Congress passes the Matthew Shepard and James Byrd Jr. Hate Crimes Prevention Act in 2009, which expands the government's ability to categorize and prosecute hate crimes.[70]

"classical" styles. Robinson is concerned that some people may only consider that as a "Black" dance owner, he would exclusively teach rap, hiphop, jazz, or other Black styles of dance, which feels like a slap in the face to him. In reality, like all people, Robinson has complexities and proficiencies in his field of expertise. Being a Black dance studio owner is part of his identity but does not tell the entirety of his human experience.

This unremitting dreamer truly went from student, collecting the shiny truths and lessons of dance and ultimately life, to teacher: "I wanted to teach all the information I have. I just want to give it to people." He expressed his own experience growing up that inspired his path in teaching. Since Robinson only had his mother in his childhood, when he met his dance instructor, that man became a father figure to him. For a young Black man, this was paramount because there was a high rate of single parent households in Black communities back then — still present today — due to social systemic causes. Ergo, Robinson states that his mentor influenced his life's purpose of becoming a teacher as a Black man. His mentor instilled into Robinson the feeling of "having my back where you don't feel like the world has your back." Now, Robinson strives to do the same for his proteges.

The question of "What am I here to do — what is my life's worth?" does not encumber the dreamers, for they do not simply feel it; they know it. Robinson is no exception. One of his many purposes is fostering an environment filled with love and warmth for his young dancers as well as older ones. "We wanted them to feel like they could have been in our home. And we made our dance studio a home for kids," Robinson said. "Maybe they had family problems at home. Or maybe they didn't feel safe at home, but you wanted to create that safe haven for those kids. So that way, although they had parents, they had us to come to if they needed anything." The spirit of Precision — that love is essential for growth, and in a world that can be unkind, there are people there for you — follows Robinson's development as a dancer and a person. And dance happens to be a bonus. Teachers nurture their pupils through feeding their souls in the pursuit of knowl-edge and creativity, but also by being harbors of security and unconditional, unrelenting love.

In a mad world, Robinson fuses dance, artistic expression, storytelling, and social justice to educate not only his students, but also our world at large. Where bigotry, -isms, and unspoken trauma run rampant, Robinson counteracts these dark sides of humanity by incorporating the subject matter into his dance routines. Truly the dreamers dream, one step at a time. "And that's what I based my dance studio on: originality and storytelling," Robinson reflected. Matters like abuse, sexual assault, racism, gun violence, and other direful topics that oftentimes feel too big for verbal communication can only be told through the body, the pain and passion that is rooted in his performers, mere children who bare their vulnerable movements to audience members. Robinson witnessed other artists' reluctance to touch on grim topics in their artistry, and he criticizes this mentality, stating his aspiration for change: "You'll have more artists willing and able and feeling able to create and bring those messages. And if you're not, if we as leaders aren't implementing and letting our kids of the future understand that those things are okay; those things are just not going to go silent. And those people who may have run into those social injustices, or felt like they were discriminated against, they're just gonna stay in silence and not have a way to voice it out. And I feel like there are people who are holding that in, and this art can help them bring that out. I think it could save lives, potentially."

Some of Robinson's dance routines include the heavy subject of domestic violence, such as the choreography he created to the X Ambassadors' song "Unsteady." The choreography opens with a mother and father arguing in front of their group of children, sitting in a circle in front of the couple. The children embark on the dance using their bodies as vessels to expound on domestic abuse.

> Robinson fuses dance, artistic expression, storytelling, and social justice to educate not only his students, but also our world at large.

2005 Hurricane Katrina strikes Louisiana. The collapse of the levee devastates low-income neighborhoods. The federal government's mismanagement of the disaster contributes to 1,800 deaths and $100 billion dollars in damages, disproportionately among Black residents. After the storm, the city becomes whiter.[71]

Robinson reveals since domestic brutality takes place away from public view, as a society we do not see the consequences it has on our children until it maladaptively manifests as they grow older: "So I took the song and I made a whole routine based on it. If you listen to that song you'll hear the lyrics incorporate how children are reacting to those things." Robinson said. "And I brought that to the stage because no one talks about those things. So if we don't shed light as artists ... the world is just going to stay the way it is. And unfortunately, the way that the world is, it is not okay."

He hopes if viewers and performers alike relate to any of the difficult topics presented, they would be able to receive help and hopefully break the stigmas that plague and divide society. He holds the responsibility of artistry very close to his heart: "Because if I can touch one person through my art, and it can carry on to someone else, then I'm doing my job in this world. So for me, I'd rather piss off five people, 20 people; but if I can make 100 people happy with my message, that means everything." Robinson is subverting the odious hush-hush topics of humanity with the beautiful and forceful art of dance, welcoming this union through dance's healing power. This is a dream come true for a Black man who has been through tribulation and still rises.

In dance and music, like many other art forms, one must hold command and control while simultaneously exposing one's innermost truths. The fear of holding back has to melt away, as Robinson expresses his visceral reactions to being an artist: "[I'm] able to feel without restriction or judgments; it helps with my vulnerability. There's times where I'm crying during a routine: I don't even know why. And it's just a part of the song that you just feel something, you go with it." This means even more to people of color. "In society nowadays, as people of color, we're supposed to be strong, and we're supposed to be headstrong, and we don't show emotions. And that's not the case for us. We are people like everybody else," Robinson said.

Emotional vulnerability through dance places Robinson in a softer light that society oftentimes doesn't allow for Black people, especially Black men. "There's different things that you're told, as a Black man — to chest up, the world's not your friend, or you have to toughen up just because of the stigma that's already placed upon your feet," he said. "As you're growing up, you're already a threat to society without having to do anything." Through dance, he is able to convey emotions that sometimes feel too big for mere words. "So with my art form, I've been able to hide behind that mostly growing up, but now as an adult, I feel more comfortable in my life, and I can say how I feel," Robinson explained. "People take that as being very aggressive. But this is just how the world is. If I didn't speak my piece, how would you know? So dance has taught me to step out of that and feel more comfortable."

Dreams are built on the dreams of other dreamers, and most parents dream of their children's futures — futures filled with freedom of self expression, abundant love, endless happiness, and the pursuit of their own dreams. Dreams that parents may never witness.

Robinson spent his life as a sempiternal dreamer, and now it is time for all children to cultivate their own lovely dreamscapes in this existence. "I want them to shoot for their dreams and understand that their parents have their backs. There's a lot of people who are dreamers, but they don't have the support. And they have to fear that this may not work for [them], instead of just embracing what they want to do," Robinson said. "I have one kid that wants to be a video gamer. Even though sometimes I know that's going to be hard for him, it's something he's passionate about. I have to support him. And I can't tell him like that's not the real world because in a world that he wants to create, he can do that. He just has to be focused."

After Robinson achieved his dance dream, he realized it was time to begin a new dream: the dream of being an engaged father. Therefore, the Robinson family moved to South Carolina, a fresh start for his children to explore and learn about their interests and for Robinson and his wife to spend time focusing on their children's development. In these fundamental years, he wants to be there for them for their sport games, dance practices, art classes, and whatever activities feed their emerging dreams.

The lofty, head-in-the-clouds mentality is often snatched away from a majority of people in youth. Few are able to retain such beautiful, dreamy ideals into adulthood. But more people can do it, with the guidance of parents and mentors who recognize that life is built on support and security to be one's authentic self, a dreamer. That is the only hope to materialize an optimistic world that is filled with love and harmony, encouraging the children we cherish so, to fly.

Robinson closes with his philosophy on supporting the dreamers: "As a dance studio owner, as a person, as a parent, that's just something you have to be willing to do. ... You just have to let them fly. And if they fly, they fly. If they fall, you just have to be there to catch them." Now do you understand us, the dreamers?

2008 In a historic election, Barack Obama (1961–) is elected the 44th president of the United States and becomes the first African American to be Commander-in-Chief

SETTING A PRECEDENT

By Jesse Marsh

Growing up in Stony Hill, a small town located on the northern outskirts of Kingston, Jamaica, Crystal Williams never had to worry about experiencing racism. She lived in a house with a yard and got to play outside without a care in the world.

After a few years living in paradise, her family migrated to New York City. To say that it was a culture shock is an understatement. She described it as almost having to change herself to fit in.

Like any Black person coming to the United States, Williams' parents made sure to warn her about how differently Americans view people of color. Looking back on the conversations, she said, "It brought about awareness about where I was." While she was always taught not to judge people based on their race, gender, or sexual orientation, she came to the realization that in America, unfortunately, people are still subjected to that mentality.

She managed to navigate her younger years in New York City successfully, but it didn't come without losing her culture in order to assimilate. Being a small, predominantly Black country, Jamaica has an incomparable community atmosphere. Jamaicans love and care for their own, and someone is always looking out to make sure young people are on the right path. Coming to a country where she was in the minority, it was hard to find people who look the same and feel the same way.

Though she started to fall out of touch with her heritage, Williams' experience as a commuter student at Temple University helped guide her back into the right direction. Though she only spent two days a week at the North Philadelphia campus, she made the most of it. Regaining her commitment to community, she did public affairs work as a communications intern for the Philadelphia Bar Association and as an external intern for the Philadelphia City Hall. There, she found her sense of belonging, having the chance to connect with people who look like her.

"I can honestly say from my heart I had a desire to be part of the community, and what attracted me to those organizations was the initiative that they were trying to project," she said. It was something she was missing in New York. Due to the time she spent trying to figure out how to be Black in America, she lost track of what made her a powerful Black woman: using her community to uplift other people who looked like her, a characteristic she developed through her immersion in Jamaican culture as a young girl.

Just as she found her footing, change got in the way again, and as a result, she had to leave Temple. "I fell deeply in love, and that caused me to leave," she said. Eventually, the relationship ended, but before she could get her education back on track, she really needed to find herself again. "After I left that relationship, I was trying to just get myself back to who I was as a person, as Christy," Williams said.

Williams has now gotten back into the swing of things with school, but not without another outside hardship threatening to derail her goals. A little over a year ago, she bought a 2014 Chevrolet Cruze from a local car dealership in Nazareth, Pennsylvania. Throughout her year of ownership, she experienced endless problems with the engine, an issue Williams continuously reported to the dealership. After consultations with her mechanic, she decided to bring it to the dealership for them to look at. Needing a car to commute to Temple, she asked for a rental, but her request was denied for what she believed was no good reason. When she decided to inquire about why she was unable to receive a rental and showed all the paperwork required to support her request, she was met with a condescending tone from the dealership employee handling her request, who said that he does not have to release a rental to her. Williams' first thought was, Why are they acting and treating me in this manner?

It seemed like she was continuously reporting her issues and following the proper protocols. Would the end result have been the same if she were a white woman? Probably not. Witnessing the situation, her colleague who accompanied her to the dealership, a white woman, was shocked at the encounter.

"She was like, 'You know, Crystal, I'm sad to say, but if you were a white woman, they would have never talked to you that way,'" Williams said.

Williams knew they discriminated against her due to her race, but she could not make a scene there. That's what people want Black folks to do. For centuries there have been stereotypes that Black people, women specifically, are boisterous and always make a big scene about everything. Williams understood that and decided to keep her composure. Instead, she did not think of herself as a victim and channeled her emotions elsewhere.

She wants to share her story with the world to ensure people understand how racism can work in multiple ways.

2016

Colin Kaepernick (1987–), an NFL quarterback for the San Francisco 49ers, begins protesting racial injustice and police brutality by sitting and later kneeling during the playing of the National Anthem at football games. Kaepernick is blacklisted by the NFL. His actions raise awareness about the police shooting deaths of Mario Woods, Philando Castile, and Anton Sterling, among others.[73] The national debate that ensues largely focuses on the appropriateness of utilizing American ideals — the American flag, the national anthem, and the military (none of which Kaepernick was protesting) — and completely ignores the issue of racial injustice.[74]

She weighs her situation in Lehigh Valley compared to her experiences in New York City: "In Lehigh Valley, it may not be as loud as New York City where racism is involved, but here I see a lot more of the covert cases, where it is more subtle, and to me that's more dangerous."

Racism is not just police brutality or redlining, but as Williams has experienced, microaggressions are a quite prominent form of racism. So how do we combat that? Williams said the most crucial thing for Black people is to refrain from staying silent: "I think we have been quiet on this issue, and it's a domino effect."

In 2020 during the social justice movement following George Floyd's murder, Black people came together and achieved real change. Historical change was ignited when former Minneapolis police officer Derek Chauvin received a 22½-year prison sentence for kneeling on Floyd's neck for eight minutes and 46 seconds. Throughout Chauvin's arrest and trial, society witnessed previously unfathomable levels of justice served to people of color. Sports teams with racist names rebranded. Multiple statues and landmarks rooted in racist history were removed.

Black people proved that if they come together, refuse to stay quiet, take action, and speak out on injustice, the nation can progress in the way that it needs to. Williams harbors a similar belief, which is why she is using her experience at the car dealership and the emotions embroiled in it to make change in the community.

Since the incident, she's become the public relations coordinator at Black Owned Known, a nonprofit organization dedicated to uplifting and unifying the Lehigh Valley community economically.

Additionally, she recently became a board member of the African American Business Leaders Council, a diversity council of the Greater Lehigh Valley Chamber of Commerce. The African American Business Leaders Council is focused on "economic empowerment [and] fostering and recognizing excellence in the African American business community." Williams' community work does not stop there as she is involved with Camel's Hump Farm, a nature education center and community garden located on the historic 135-acre Archibald Johnson estate, the country home of Bethlehem's first mayor.

Looking beyond the Lehigh Valley, she has plans to move back to Jamaica to start multiple nonprofit organizations as homage to the community-building traits she learned there as a mechanism to cope with racism.

Despite Williams' dehumanizing car dealership experience, as a result of her community involvement, she has a positive outlook for the future of Black people in the Lehigh Valley area. "You can't go into wanting to see change with a

Crystal Williams, Public Relations Coordinator at Black Owned Known, compares her lived experiences in Jamaica, New York City, and the Lehigh Valley. Bethlehem, Pa., Sept. 5, 2021. (Writing Wrongs/Shannon O'Connor)

pessimistic mindset." she said. "Sometimes you do have to see the beauty in the ashes, and sometimes some shields will have to burn for you to get those ashes."

Ultimately, she hopes her story can show Black people that they are not alone when they experience microaggressions and that joining community organizations is a medium to use their voices to make a change: "I feel like it'll bring awareness, and it will take away the self-doubt that a lot of Black people go through when they experience these things."

With people like Williams using their experiences to be active in the community, there is optimism for progress in the near future. She is a leader for people of color in the area and knows not to let a racist encounter tear her down because that's what the racists want. Williams uses microaggressions aimed towards her as motivation to empower future generations in the hope that they will not have to deal with the injustices she and numerous others have endured.

2020 The murder of George Floyd (1973–2020) at the hands of Minneapolis police officer Derek Chauvin ignites rage about continued police brutality. Despite the COVID-19 Pandemic, Americans participate in protests and riots.[75]

2021 Kamala Harris (1964–) is sworn in as vice president of the United States, becoming the first woman and the second person of color (Black/Asian) to hold this office.[76]

BLACK LIVES MATTER

Illustration by Veronika Hammond, Ian Long, and Kelly Sulca Hernandez

IN MEMORY OF THE COUNTLESS VICTIMS OF POLICE BRUTALITY

Front row, left to right: Philando Castile, Botham Jean, Ahmaud Arbery, Elijah McClain, Freddie Gray, Trayvon Martin, Tamir Rice, Atatiana Jefferson
Second row, left to right: Oscar Grant, Michael Brown Jr., Eric Garner, George Floyd, Terence Crutcher, Sandra Bland, Walter Scott, Daunte Wright
Third Row: Breonna Taylor, Ronald Greene

2021 WRITING WRONGS STAFF

Writing & Editing

Milena Berestko
Lafayette College

Sonjirose Chin
Borough of Manhattan Community College

Tiersa Curry
Kutztown University

Natalie Dang
California State University, Los Angeles

Shanaé Harte
CUNY York College

Ben Hopper
Ramapo College

Jesse Marsh
Villanova University

Luka Marjanovic
Ramapo College

Heather Moran
Temple University

Ebube Nwaeme
Borough of Manhattan Community College

Chekwube Okunowo
Drew University

Cat Oriel
George Washington University

Rohail Spear
Franklin & Marshall College

Doris Turkel
SUNY Binghamton University

2021 WRITING WRONGS STAFF

Design & Illustration

VERONIKA HAMMOND
Montclair State University

IAN LONG
Montclair State University

KELLY SULCA HERNANDEZ
Northampton Community College

Photography

JENNIFER BERRIOS
Ursinus College

ALLIANA MYERS
Temple University

SHANNON O'CONNOR
Montclair State University

Videography

KYLIE STOLTZFUS
Millersville University

Social Media Management

ALEXIS JACQUET
Borough of Manhattan Community College

SERAFINA KENNEDY
Rutgers University

2021 WRITING WRONGS ADVISORS

Dawn Heinbach
Founder & President/CEO, Writing Wrongs

Independent Multimedia Journalist
Kutztown, Pa.

Nina Renna
Assistant Coordinator

Owner, Tactile Designs
Philadelphia, Pa.

* WW 2018 Staff Designer

Design & Illustration

Gayle Hendricks
Instructor,
Northampton Community College
Northampton, Pa.

Videography & Social Media Management

Sydney Herdle
Digital Media Producer, University of Connecticut
Sydney Herdle Photography & Multimedia,
Manchester, Conn.
* WW 2018 Staff Photographer

Photography

Jennifer Grima
Owner, Jen Grima Photograph
Macungie, Pa.

Writing/Editing

Kimberlee Bongard
Associate Producer, NJPBS
Newark, N.J.
* WW 2019 Staff Writer

Writing/Editing

Steven Hernandez
Ph.D. candidate, Philosophy
CUNY Graduate Center, New York, N.Y.
Instructor, City College of New York
* WW 2019 Staff Writer

Writing/Editing

Justin Sweitzer
Managing Editor, City & State P
Harrisburg, Pa.
* WW 2016 Staff Writer
* WW 2017 Staff Designer

Front row, from left: Tiersa Curry, Heather Moran, Ian Long, Serafina Kennedy, Luka Marjanovic, Milena Berestko
Middle row (seated), from left: Kylie Stoltzfus, Sonjirose Chin, Cat Oriel, Doris Turkel, Natalie Dang, Alliana Myers
Top row, from left: Veronika Hammond, Shanaé Harte, Chekwube Okunowo, Jesse Marsh, Ebube Nwaeme, Rohail Spear, Alexis Jacquet, Ben Hopper, Kelly Sulca Hernandez, Jennifer Berrios, Shannon O'Connor
Bethlehem, Pa., Sept. 5, 2021. (Writing Wrongs/Alliana Myers)

Writing Wrongs is an advocacy journalism project that illuminates the inequity in our society through the power of the pen and the lens. By telling the stories of those directly affected by social issues, Writing Wrongs offers a different and often-ignored perspective that challenges stereotypes and prejudices.

College students who are accepted into the annual program spend Labor Day weekend at a specific location and immerse themselves in a specific societal issue. They perform interviews, take pictures and videos, manage and update our social media, and ultimately design a print file that is then published. The goal of raising awareness is accomplished by donating the student-created book to local and regional public and college libraries and relevant organizations. The books are also available world-wide through online book sellers.

67 WRITING WRONGS

— SUSTAINING SPONSOR —

Townsend Press

"Helping you help students learn."

K-12, Basic Skills/ESL, College

Townsend Press is an independent publisher of acclaimed English/Language Arts materials for students in elementary school through college.

We are committed to helping students develop the reading, writing, and language skills needed for success in the classroom and beyond. We want to help students thrive.

We're Independent.
Our Materials Work.
We're Focused.
We Give Back.

www.townsendpress.com   cs@townsendpress.com
(800) 772-6410
439 Kelley Drive, West Berlin, NJ 08091-9164

THANK YOU!

— Friend Sponsors —

Alexyss Panfile   Sydney Herdle

— Justice Sponsors —

Charles & Jane Kerschner

Designers and illustrators begin working on the 2021 edition of the book. From left: Kelly Sulca Hernandez, Veronika Hammond, Ian Long. Bethlehem, Pa., Sept. 4, 2021. (Writing Wrongs/Gayle F. Hendricks)

NOTES

1. Gilder Lehrman Institute of American History, A Spotlight on a Primary Source by Christopher Columbus, "Columbus Reports on His First Voyage, 1493," accessed December 19, 2023, https://www.gilderlehrman.org/history-resources/spotlight-primary-source/columbus-reports-his-first-voyage-1493.
2. Sherburne F. Cook and Woodrow Borah, "The Aboriginal Population of Hispaniola," essay, in Essays in Population History: Mexico and the Caribbean (Berkeley, CA: University of California Press, 1971), 376–410.
3. Mark Cartwright, "Juan Ponce de León," World History Encyclopedia, July 12, 2022, https://www.worldhistory.org/Juan_Ponce_de_Leon/.
4. Amy Tikkanen, "Hernando de Soto," Encyclopædia Britannica, December 14, 2023, https://www.britannica.com/biography/Hernando-de-Soto.
5. McCartney, Martha, "John Smith (Bap. 1580–1631)." Encyclopedia Virginia, December 22, 2021. https://encyclopediavirginia.org/entries/smith-john-bap-1580-1631/.
6. Rountree, Helen C. "Pocahontas (d. 1617)." Encyclopedia Virginia, November 14, 2023. https://encyclopediavirginia.org/entries/pocahontas-d-1617/.
7. Beth Austin, rep., 1619: Virginia's First Africans (Hampton History Museum, December 2019), https://hampton.gov/DocumentCenter/View/24075/1619-Virginias-First-Africans?bidId=.
8. Khushbu Shah and Juweek Adolphe, "400 Years since Slavery: A Timeline of American History," The Guardian, August 16, 2019, https://www.theguardian.com/news/2019/aug/15/400-years-since-slavery-timeline.
9. Meg Matthias, ed., "French and Indian War," Encyclopædia Britannica, December 1, 2023, https://www.britannica.com/event/French-and-Indian-War.
10. Steven Mintz, "The Gilder Lehrman Institute of American History," Historical Context: The Constitution and Slavery | Gilder Lehrman Institute of American History, accessed November 22, 2023, https://www.gilderlehrman.org/history-resources/teaching-resource/historical-context-constitution-and-slavery.
11. Ariela Gross and David R. Upham, "Article IV, Section 2: Movement of Persons throughout the Union," National Constitution Center – constitutioncenter.org, accessed December 3, 2023, https://constitutioncenter.org/the-constitution/articles/article-iv/clauses/37.
12. Ariela Gross and David R. Upham, "Article IV, Section 2: Movement of Persons throughout the Union," National Constitution Center – constitutioncenter.org, accessed December 3, 2023, https://constitutioncenter.org/the-constitution/articles/article-iv/clauses/37.
13. Washington W. Irving, "The Sacagawea Mystique: Her Age, Name Role and Final Destiny," Columbia Magazine (Washington State Historical Society, 1999), https://www.washingtonhistory.org/wp-content/uploads/2020/04/sacagawea-mystique.pdf.
14. National Archives, "The Slave Trade: The Act Prohibiting the Importation of Slaves, 1808," The U.S. National Archives and Records Administration, January 7, 2022, https://www.archives.gov/education/lessons/slave-trade.html.
15. Henry Louis Gates, "How Many Slaves Landed in the US?," The Root, January 6, 2014, https://www.theroot.com/how-many-slaves-landed-in-the-us-1790873989.
16. Joseph C.G. Kennedy, introduction, in Population of the United States in 1960 (Washington, DC: Bureau of the Census Library, 1864), xii.12. https://www.census.gov/library/publications/1864/dec/1860a.html
17. Debra Buchholtz, "Reservations," essay, in Encyclopedia of United States Indian Policy and Law, ed. Paul Finkelman and Tim A. Garrison (Washington, D.C.: CQ Press, 2009), 668–74, https://doi.org/10.4135/9781604265767.
18. Charles Reagan Wilson and Willam R. Ferris, "Frederick Douglass, 1818-1895," essay, in Encyclopedia of Southern Culture (Chapel Hill u.a., NC: Univ. of North Carolina Press, 1989).
19. "A Nation's Story: 'What to the Slave Is the Fourth of July?'" National Museum of African American History and Culture, July 2, 2022. https://nmaahc.si.edu/explore/stories/nations-story-what-slave-fourth-july.
20. Adam Zeidan, ed., "Mexican-American War," Encyclopædia Britannica, November 6, 2023, https://www.britannica.com/event/Mexican-American-War.
21. Michals, Debra, ed. "Harriet Tubman Biography." National Women's History Museum, n.d. https://www.womenshistory.org/education-resources/biographies/harriet-tubman.
22. Debra Buchholtz, "Reservations," essay, in Encyclopedia of United States Indian Policy and Law, ed. Paul Finkelman and Tim A. Garrison (Washington, D.C.: CQ Press, 2009), 668–74, https://doi.org/10.4135/9781604265767.
23. Melvin I. Urofsky, "Dred Scott Decision," Encyclopædia Britannica, November 7, 2023, https://www.britannica.com/event/Dred-Scott-decision.
24. Augustyn, Adam. "First Battle of Bull Run." Encyclopedia Britannica, July 14, 2023. https://www.britannica.com/event/First-Battle-of-Bull-Run-1861.
25. "The Emancipation Proclamation," National Archives, January 28, 2022, https://www.archives.gov/exhibits/featured-documents/emancipation-proclamation#:~:text=President%20Abraham%20Lincoln%20issued%20the,and%20henceforward%20shall%20be%20free.%22.
26. Meg Matthias, ed., "Emancipation Proclamation [United States 1863]," Encyclopædia Britannica, October 20, 2023, https://www.britannica.com/event/Emancipation-Proclamation.

27. Stejskal, James. "The Jayhawker and the Conductor: The Combahee Ferry Raid, 2 June 1863." The Army Historical Foundation, June 18, 2022. https://armyhistory.org/the-jayhawker-and-the-conductor-the-combahee-ferry-raid-2-june-1863/.
28. Service, Joe. "The Surrender Meeting." National Parks Service, June 14, 2022. https://www.nps.gov/apco/learn/historyculture/the-surrender-meeting.htm.
29. 13th Amendment to the U.S. Constitution: Abolition of Slavery (1865)." National Archives and Records Administration, May 10, 2022. https://www.archives.gov/milestone-documents/13th-amendment.
30. Tracy Grant, ed., "Juneteenth," Encyclopædia Britannica, October 19, 2023, https://www.britannica.com/topic/Juneteenth.
31. Vanessa Holloway and Vanessa Holloway, "Initial Legal Barriers to Racial Equality, 1865–1868," essay, in Black Rights in the Reconstruction Era (Lanham, MD: Hamilton Books, 2018), 2–3.
32. McVeigh, Rory, and Kevin Estep. "The Ku Klux Klan in American History." In The Politics of Losing: Trump, the Klan, and the Mainstreaming of Resentment, 19–54. Columbia University Press, 2019. http://www.jstor.org/stable/10.7312/mcve19006.4.
33. Adam Augustyn, ed., "Fourteenth Amendment," Encyclopædia Britannica, November 25, 2023, https://www.britannica.com/topic/Fourteenth-Amendment.
34. "15th Amendment to the U.S. Constitution: Voting Rights (1870)," National Archives and Records Administration, February 8, 2022, https://www.archives.gov/milestone-documents/15th-amendment.
35. Melvin I. Urofsky, "Jim Crow Law," Encyclopædia Britannica, November 21, 2023, https://www.britannica.com/event/Jim-Crow-law.
36. Janet A. McDonnell, introduction, in The Dispossession of the American Indian, 1887-1934 (Bloomington: Indiana University Press, 1991), 1–5.
37. Myles Hudson, "Wounded Knee Massacre," Encyclopædia Britannica, February 27, 2023, https://www.britannica.com/event/Wounded-Knee-Massacre.
38. "Plessy v. Ferguson (1896)," National Archives and Records Administration, February 8, 2022, https://www.archives.gov/milestone-documents/plessy-v-ferguson.
39. Scot Ngozi-Brown, "African-American Soldiers and Filipinos: Racial Imperialism, Jim Crow and Social Relations," The Journal of Negro History 82, no. 1 (Winter 1997): 42–53, https://doi.org/10.2307/2717495.
40. Jeff Wallenfeldt, "National Association for the Advancement of Colored People," Encyclopædia Britannica, November 20, 2023, https://www.britannica.com/topic/National-Association-for-the-Advancement-of-Colored-People.
41. Jeff Wallenfeldt, ed., "Great Migration," Encyclopædia Britannica, November 2, 2023, https://www.britannica.com/event/Great-Migration.
42. Scott Ellsworth, "Tulsa Race Massacre," "Tulsa Race Massacre," The Encyclopedia of Oklahoma History and Culture, accessed December 1, 2023, https://www.okhistory.org/publications/enc/entry.php?entry=TU013.
43. Danney Goble, rep., Tulsa Race Riot: A Report by the Oklahoma Commission to Study the Tulsa Race Riot of 1921 (Tulsa, OK: Oklahoma Commission to Study the Tulsa Race Riot of 1921, 2001).
44. 1. Henry Goldschmidt, Elizabeth A. McAlister, and Jennifer Snow, "The Civilization of White Men: The Race of the Hindu in United States v. Bhagat Singh Thind," essay, in Race, Nation, and Religion in the Americas (New York, NY: Oxford University Press, 2004), 259–80.
45. "Records of Rights," Native American Citizenship, 1924, accessed December 11, 2023, http://recordsofrights.org/events/93/native-american-citizenship.
46. "Senate Leaders," U.S. Senate: Senate Leaders, August 7, 2023, https://www.senate.gov/about/origins-foundations/parties-leadership/curtis-charles.htm.
47. Amy Tikkanen, ed., "Tuskegee Syphilis Study," Encyclopædia Britannica, November 6, 2023, https://www.britannica.com/event/Tuskegee-syphilis-study.
48. Michael Ray, ed., "Tuskegee Airmen," Encyclopædia Britannica, December 2, 2023, https://www.britannica.com/topic/Tuskegee-Airmen.
49. Michael Ray, ed., "Code Talker," Encyclopædia Britannica, November 23, 2023, https://www.britannica.com/topic/code-talker.
50. Hinnershitz, Stephanie Ph.D. "The Zoot Suit Riots and Wartime Los Angeles." The National World War II Museum New Orleans. The National World War II Museum New Orleans, June 1, 2023. https://www.nationalww2museum.org/war/articles/zoot-suit-riots-and-wartime-los-angeles
51. Rick Livingston, ed., "Atomic Bombings of Hiroshima and Nagasaki," Encyclopædia Britannica, December 7, 2023, https://www.britannica.com/event/atomic-bombings-of-Hiroshima-and-Nagasaki.
52. "Buffalo Soldiers in the Korean War," National Parks Service, June 28, 2023, https://www.nps.gov/chyo/learn/historyculture/busokoreanwar.htm.
53. "Brown v. Board of Education (1954)," National Archives and Records Administration, November 22, 2021, https://www.archives.gov/milestone-documents/brown-v-board-of-education.
54. "Emmett Till." FBI, May 18, 2016. https://www.fbi.gov/history/famous-cases/emmett-till.
55. "Little Rock School Desegregation." The Martin Luther King, Jr. Research and Education Institute, Stanford University. Accessed December 7, 2023. https://kinginstitute.stanford.edu/little-rock-school-desegregation.
56. Michals, Debra, Ph.D. "Biography: Ruby Bridges." National Women's History Museum. Accessed December 7, 2023. https://www.womenshistory.org/education-resources/biographies/ruby-bridges.

57. Holmes, Marian Smith. "The Freedom Riders, Then and Now." Smithsonian Magazine, Smithsonian.com, February 1, 2009. https://www.smithsonianmag.com/history/the-freedom-riders-then-and-now-45351758/.

58. David L. Lewis, "The Letter from the Birmingham Jail of Martin Luther King, Jr..," Encyclopædia Britannica, accessed December 9, 2023, https://www.britannica.com/biography/Martin-Luther-King-Jr/The-letter-from-the-Birmingham-jail.

59. Zarr, Christopher. "Martin Luther King, Jr.." National Archives at New York City, February 2, 2022. https://www.archives.gov/nyc/exhibit/mlk.

60. "Malcolm X." The Martin Luther King, Jr. Research and Education Institute, Stanford University. Accessed December 7, 2023. https://kinginstitute.stanford.edu/malcolm-x.

61. "Legal Highlight: The Civil Rights Act of 1964." United States Department of Labor. Accessed December 7, 2023. https://www.dol.gov/agencies/oasam/civil-rights-center/statutes/civil-rights-act-of-1964#:~:text=In%201964%2C%20Congress%20passed%20Public,hiring%2C%20promoting%2C%20and%20firing.

62. "Selma Marches," National Archives and Records Administration, August 8, 2022, https://www.archives.gov/research/african-americans/vote/selma-marches.

63. Will Elsbury, "Racial, Ethnic, and Religious Minorities in the Vietnam War: A Resource Guide: Introduction," Research Guides at Library of Congress, September 12, 2022, https://guides.loc.gov/racial-ethnic-and-religious-minorities-in-the-vietnam-war.

64. "Immigration and Nationality Act of 1965." US House of Representatives: History, Art & Archives. Accessed December 7, 2023. https://history.house.gov/Historical-Highlights/1951-2000/Immigration-and-Nationality-Act-of-1965/.

65. Anne L. Foster, "War on Drugs Declared," essay, in The Long War on Drugs (Durham, NC: Duke University Press, 2023), 109–21. https://doi.org/10.2307/jj.8441764.15

66. Diana E. Murphy, et. al., 2002 Report to the Congress: Federal Cocaine Sentencing Policy (United States Sentencing Commission, May 2002), https://www.ussc.gov/sites/default/files/pdf/news/congressional-testimony-and-reports/drug-topics/200205-rtc-cocaine-sentencing-policy/Ch5.pdf.

67. Craig Reinarman and Harry G. Levine, "Crack in the Rearview Mirror: Deconstructing Drug War Mythology." Social Justice 31 (1/2 (95-96)): 182–99. Social Justice 31.5, no. 95–96 (January 2004): 182–99, https://www.jstor.org/stable/29768248.

68. Robert Moran et al., "Move Bombing in Philadelphia," https://www.inquirer.com, accessed December 9, 2023, https://www.inquirer.com/move-bombing/.

69. Anjuli Sastry Krbechek and Karen Grigsby Bates, "When La Erupted in Anger: A Look Back at the Rodney King Riots," NPR WITF, April 26, 2017, https://www.npr.org/2017/04/26/524744989/when-la-erupted-in-anger-a-look-back-at-the-rodney-king-riots.

70. Campbell Robertson, "Texas Executes White Supremacist for 1998 Dragging Death of James Byrd Jr..," The New York Times, April 24, 2019, https://www.nytimes.com/2019/04/24/us/james-byrd-jr-john-william-king.html.

71. Elizabeth Fussell, Narayan Sastry, and Mark VanLandingham, "Race, Socioeconomic Status, and Return Migration to New Orleans after Hurricane Katrina," Population and Environment 31, no. 1–3 (January 2010): 20–42, https://doi.org/10.1007/s11111-009-0092-2.

72. "Barack Obama." The White House, December 23, 2022. https://www.whitehouse.gov/about-the-white-house/presidents/barack-obama/.

73. Dylan Shulman, "Colin Kaepernick," Encyclopædia Britannica, November 23, 2023, https://www.britannica.com/biography/Colin-Kaepernick.

74. Shane M. Graber, Ever J. Figueroa, and Krishnan Vasudevan, "Oh, Say, Can You Kneel: A Critical Discourse Analysis of Newspaper Coverage of Colin Kaepernick's Racial Protest," Howard Journal of Communications 31, no. 5 (September 26, 2019): 464–80, https://doi.org/10.1080/10646175.2019.1670295.

75. The New York Times. "How George Floyd Died, and What Happened Next." The New York Times, September 8, 2020. https://www.nytimes.com/article/george-floyd.html.

76. "Kamala Harris: The Vice President." The White House, August 28, 2023. https://www.whitehouse.gov/administration/vice-president-harris/.

Printed in the USA
CPSIA information can be obtained
at www.ICGtesting.com
LVHW082154030424
776152LV00009B/207